$L280$

COMPUTERS, RECORDS AND THE RIGHT TO PRIVACY

The record of a Conference held on 24 and 25 January 1979, organised by the Institute of Data Processing Management, the National Computing Centre Ltd and the National Council for Civil Liberties.

Edited by Patricia Hewitt

INPUT TWO-NINE LTD

First published in the United Kingdom in 1979 by Input Two-Nine Ltd., 7 Banstead Road, Purley, Surrey CR2 3ER.

ISBN 0 905897 27 7   Input Two-Nine Ltd

Printed in Sweden
Studentlitteratur
Lund 1979.

PREFACE

On 24 and 25 January 1979, the National Council for Civil Liberties, together with the Institute of Data Processing Management and the National Computing Centre Ltd., convened a Conference on Computers, Records and the Right to Privacy.

The main purpose of the Conference was to debate the report of the Data Protection Committee and to learn from the experience of privacy legislation in the United States of America, Sweden and other Western European countries.

It is over ten years since NCCL launched the privacy campaign with a publication in 1968, which concluded that 'the time for action is *now*'. In 1970, when NCCL organised a two-day Workshop on the Data Bank Society, it was clear that the threat of increasingly sophisticated data banks was real and growing, and that legislation was needed. But it was not until the end of 1975 — three years after the Younger Committee on Privacy reported — that the Government published its White Papers on computers and privacy and established a Data Protection Committee to advise on the details of the legislation required.

Growing concern with movements of data between countries, and the proposed Council of Europe Convention on data processing, combined with the report of the Data Protection Committee, make it inevitable that legislation will be achieved in the United Kingdom, at least before 1984. As this report shows, the Conference participants — representing a very wide range of organisations and interests — were generally agreed on the need for legislation as soon as possible, and welcomed the Data Protection Committee's report as providing an appropriate basis for data protection.

It was also clear at the Conference that there was widespread support for the view that legislation should extend beyond computerised records to include manually-held records. Much of the most sensitive personal data held on individuals at present — social work and medical records, school records, many personnel records — are not computerised and may not be for some years. But, as the Data Protection Committee report stressed, the principles of data protection apply regardless of whether or not the information is automatically processed.

This book contains both the background papers presented to the Conference and a report of the speeches and discussion. Although contributions have had to be edited, the book does, we believe, faithfully reflect the views of the speakers and participants.

We should like to thank all those who made the Conference the success it was. Our co-sponsors, who provided considerable support, were ASTMS, AUEW (TASS), the British Medical Association, CPSA, MIND (the National Association for Mental Health), Anthony McNulty, Director of the British Institute of Human Rights, and NALGO. We are particularly grateful to those who served on the Conference steering committee: Edward Cluff (Institute of Data Processing Management), Dr. Jo Hanlon, Joe Jacob (Lecturer in Law, London School of Economics), Rory Johnston (*Computer Weekly*), James Michael (Lecturer in Law, Polytechnic of Central London), Hugh Pitcher (National Computing Centre Ltd), Alan Simpson (IDPM), William Birtles (NCCL Executive Committee Member), Michael Fluskey (Input Two-Nine Ltd) and Elizabeth Jones (Conference Organiser).

Unfortunately, the Home Secretary, the Rt. Hon. Merlyn Rees, was barred by political and industrial problems from attending the Conference and we were most grateful to Lord Boston, Minister of State at the Home Office, for stepping in at the last minute and delivering his speech. We were also very sorry indeed to lose Ms Kerstin Aner, from the Swedish Ministry of Education, and Christopher Layton, from the EEC, both of whom were trapped by appalling weather conditions. We have, however, included Ms Aner's speech in this report. We were particularly grateful to Russell Pipe, Editor of *Transnational Data Report*, and Roy Harrington from the Home Office, who stepped in at the last minute to talk about developments within the OECD and the Council of Europe.

Finally, we should like to express our warmest thanks to Elizabeth Jones, the Conference Organiser, whose calm efficiency and dedication ensured its smooth and successful running.

Patricia Hewitt,
General Secretary, National Council for Civil Liberties.

CONTENTS

Section 1

INFORMATION PRIVACY: AN OVERVIEW

Rt Hon David Steel MP, Leader of the Liberal Party

I am very privileged to be invited to open this important conference. A science fiction story called *Answer*, written by Frederick Bryan some time ago might be an appropriate preface to my remarks and to the rest of your deliberations. The time is in the far distant future when the heads of the numerous inter-galactic federations meet for the inaugural linking together of all the computers on myriads of planets. There is, of course, inter-galactic network television coverage of the event. The President of the Universe solemnly throws the switch linking the systems together and he then steps forward to make the initial ceremonial interrogation previously selected by a panel of the wisest men from every galaxy. 'Is there a god?' he asks. And after a millisecond's pause the computer replies, 'There is now!' The President leaps forward to switch off the machine, but before he reaches the switch, a bolt of lightning strikes him dead.

Well, Mr Chairman, whether divine retribution has yet been quantified by finite algorithm and whether it is a real risk to be run when tackling such subjects as computers, records and the right to privacy, remains to be seen. But whatever the risks involved, we must face such subjects squarely, and the time is certainly right for a conference such as this.

Although it is not of immediate concern to the work of this conference, a revolution is taking place across the whole field of communications. The enhanced technological capability that we now have at our disposal poses questions of fundamental importance for decision-takers and legislators. What is at stake is nothing less than the distribution of power within our society on the one hand, and the psychological integrity of the individual on the other. In *Information Technology* in 1972 Theodore Louis wrote this:

> "We assume a direct linkage between information and politics based on a definition of information as 'a resource convertible to political power'. All resources, human and physical, influence the commitments of decision makers and the composition of elite groups in the social structure, but politics is especially sensitive to information and to significant variations in the amount and character of available information."

The power elite that could result if Louis is correct would be administrative and managerial rather than political. It would result in a diminution of the real and effective power of politicians and elected representatives. When, for example, cable television, with its two-way facility, becomes a reality and the electorate is able to be consulted and can be instantly called upon to register its opinion on any question, the political realities will be quite different from those that prevail today. If, for example, the one to three million television sets in Scotland had been consulted before the Second Reading of the Scotland Bill, I think the resultant Act with its referendum would very likely have been quite different, and under circumstances such as these our present system of delegated democracy could become transformed into a meritocracy in which power will reside in a superior ability to make use of the existing technology.

That is why I wholeheartedly endorse the recent plea made by my colleague, Eric Avebury, in his address to the Australian Computer Society for an international centre to study the effects of information technology on society and to disseminate information about this to the world's decision-makers. Such a body is essential in order that knowledge about these important effects can be compiled continuously rather than in fits and starts, as with the *ad hoc* studies currently being carried out in different countries.

Of more direct concern perhaps to the work of this conference is the growth of institutionalised bureaucracy. As Haslett reminded us, 'corporate bodies are more corrupt and profligate than individuals because they have more power to do mischief and are less amenable to disgrace or punishment. They feel neither shame, remorse, gratitude nor good will. The principle of private and natural conscience is extinguished in each individual and nothing is considered but how the united efforts of the whole may be best directed to obtaining political advantages and privileges to be shared as common spoil. Each member reaps the benefit and lays the blame, if there is any, on the rest'.

The technology available to us today would bewilder any time traveller from Haslett's day, but the ideas of De Tocqueville, Mill and Spencer, although in need of re-interpretation, are still I think as relevant today. How much regulation, even in the cause of virtue, can man and society bear and still retain individual liberty and independence? the burgeoning bureaucracies of both government and big business are organisations which are increasingly dependent on the idiot rationality of machines. The range of intrusion of the state is infinitely greater; the scrutiny is more detailed and the knowledge more perfect than ever before. And so the gap between the governors and the governed increases, and the hiatus poses a threat to the health and stability of our systems of government.

Against this background of the communications revolution and the increase of bureaucracy, I should like to turn to the concept of privacy and, if I may, for a moment consider it on its own before considering those particular aspects related to computers and records. A great deal has been said and written in recent years about privacy. In particular, I am indebted to Maurice Cranston's recent Elliott Dodds Lecture delivered at Leeds University, called 'The right to privacy'. The text of that repays careful study. Professor Cranston asserts that privacy is a relatively modern term, and he traces its origins to an article in the Harvard Law Review in December 1890 called 'The right to privacy'. It claimed in effect that there already existed a right to privacy enshrined in the common law, but that the right to privacy in the sense of a right upheld by the courts and enjoyed by the citizen had yet to be effectively instituted.

That statement made 90 years ago is still apt to the situation that obtains now in this country and adds urgency to the deliberations of gatherings such as this.

There are, in fact, at least three different interpretations which can attach to the idea of a right. First, there exists in many countries of the world formal legal rights which may be enshrined in high-flown, highly principled, written constitutions. In these same countries, government is carried on by dictatorships and other repressive regimes, and so these formal, legal rights and guarantees are honoured only in their breach.

3

Secondly, there are positive legal rights. A positive legal protection of the right to privacy would result in a tort or delict occurring where privacy was invaded and would therefore constitute a breach in the law for which an injured party could seek redress in the civil courts. Thirdly, there are what could be called 'social rights'. A social right is one that is upheld, not by formal penalties of legal institutions, but by the informal sanction of public opinion, an unwritten law sustained by what John Stuart Mill called 'society itself'.

In passing, it may be worth noting that Professor Cranston, in a review of the American cases, found that the claim that American courts recognised any positive legal right to privacy did not stand up to serious scrutiny. American courts only upheld the right to privacy when it was co-joined with another right or interest, but when privacy by itself was at stake the courts did not recognise it.

It may also be worth noting that the idea of obtaining redress by a public court of an invasion of privacy does seem slightly absurd and a contradiction in itself, since the method of redress could compound the original offence. There has been an assumption that the right to privacy is a kind of bourgeois privilege which has been put in jeopardy by the rise of a more egalitarian society, but it needs to be noticed, in this connection, that the right to privacy is, in my view, now more important in poorer homes when, for example, social security inspectors seek to enter them in order to establish whether a mother receiving benefit is co-habiting with a male who has adequate means of supporting her.

So, if we leave to one side the positive right to privacy within the civil code as a possible sanction, we must look to see how criminal and administrative law can provide the protection that we seek. The main purpose of legislation of this kind would be to locate and then control threats to privacy. I suggest that the NCCL's own four key points serve this purpose quite well as a framework:

— that legislation should direct the way in which personal information may be gathered;

— that it should proscribe the use of inaccurate, out-of-date or irrelevant information or opinions as the basis of decisions;

— that it should make inadequate security of confidential information an offence;

— that it should regulate the transfer of information given for one purpose without the individual's consent.

These provisions should apply equally to files held in manilla folders as well as to the most sophisticated, full text retrieval, computerised systems. On top of all this, it is only right that we should not give the Government

4

complete protection of unchecked access to our lives through outdated and oppressive legislation. This is why I applaud my colleague, Clement Freud, in using his allocation of a Private Member's Bill to introduce an Official Information Bill, to which I am glad to say the House of Commons gave an unopposed Second Reading last week.

As I attempted to demonstrate at the beginning, the impact of computers and the communications industry on our society, together with the attendant problems of institutionalisation and the erosion of our personal privacy, can be treated as separate subjects. But they merit particular consideration when brought together. The Younger Report on Privacy, published in 1972, eventually resulted in the White Paper published in December 1975 on Computers and Privacy. That White Paper announced the Government's intention to appoint the Data Protection Committee, which, under your chairmanship, Mr Chairman, reported in December last year.

Anyone who studies this rather massive and formidable report must be impressed, first of all, by its lucidity and range. I think all the committee members certainly earned their right to sign that report. They produced an odyssey through the uncharted seas of data protection and have established landmarks for all who follow them. In the context of proposed international co-operation, the report says that British legislation should be speeded up. Indeed, this is a masterly understatement, because some experts are now predicting that in the United States in just over five years comprehensive information on all citizens will be stored in a central national databank. And against prophesies like that we in the United Kingdom surely dally at our peril.

Having said that I was impressed by your report, sir, I have also to say that, in my opinion, it does not go quite far enough. The key paragraph is no. 2 on the first page, where it states:

"The function of a data protection law should be different from that of a law on privacy. Rather than establishing rights, it should provide a framework for finding the balance of interest of the individual, the data user and the community at large."

I appreciate the reasons which led the committee to that conclusion, but I hope that this conference does not feel itself bound within that particular constraint. That point of view would produce legislation that is much less direct than that already existing in other countries. The United States, France and Sweden have all, for example, laid down statutory rights for access for people to inspect information held about them, though exempting areas such as national security. I was pleased last year to be able to meet Mrs Aner from Stockholm — the minister who will be attending this conference — and to discuss the Swedish legislation with her. It has had its problems. But the Lindop Committee concluded that this statutory right is not flexible enough because of the widely differing ways that computer systems operate.

I am inclined to disagree with them. The approach of your committee, sir, may be contrasted with the more thoroughgoing conclusions of the United States study commission *Personal privacy in an information society* which reported in July 1977. That commission stated that three objectives were intrinsic to effective privacy safeguards:

1) to minimise intrusion, to create a proper balance between what an individual is expected to divulge to a record-keeping organisation and what he or she seeks in return;

2) to maximise fairness, to open up record-keeping operations in ways that will minimise the extent to which recorded information about an individual is itself a source of unfairness where it is used to make a decision;

3) to create legitimate enforceable expectations of confidentiality, to create and define obligations with respect to the uses and disclosures that will be made of recorded information about an individual.

That type of approach, I would argue, is far more fundamental than the Lindop Committee's conclusions, and it accords very much more with the NCCL's own view, and would, among other things, guarantee the individual's right to see, to copy and to correct his record. The United States commission also put the onus on record-keepers to limit data collected to that which is necessary.

I am aware that the United States commission decided against an omnibus privacy law. It preferred legislation drawn up industry by industry within a general framework of rights and obligations.

I also hope that this conference will not restrict itself to automated invasions of privacy, and I take it that the word 'record' inserted into the conference title will allow you to delve into the manilla folders as well as the computer software systems. I was disappointed that the Data Protection Committee's terms of reference did not in fact admit manual systems, and it is slightly ludicrous that the Consumer Credit Act of 1974 has already gone further in this direction by giving people the right to see and correct information held on them by credit reference agencies, whether they are in IBM boxes or orange boxes.

I am also extremely concerned by the implications of the interlocking of state data banks. A recent article in the *Sunday Times* revealed the fact that information supplied in the course of applying for a vehicle licence is passed to the central police computer. This is not mentioned to the applicant anywhere in the application form. The Customs and Excise Departments also have access to the Swansea computer banks, and apparently information also reaches the Inland Revenue and the Home Office. Certainly Parliament has never authorised any such schemes. They are simply the result of administrative decisions.

The benefits of such an interchange are plainly obvious, but the disadvantages less obvious but nonetheless potentially pernicious. And as the prospect of the universal person identifier — upi — becomes more real, Parliament as a whole surely has to face up to the consequences of such developments.

As I have said, the Lindop Committee conclusions in general did not go far enough for me, and I suspect that the legislation will not come fast enough either. The Lindop Committee members were impressed by the speed at which the picture had changed in the period since the Younger Report in 1972, and I agree with them. The Lindop Committee Report is an attempt to bring the British law up to date, and I sincerely hope that the subject will be treated with the urgency that it deserves.

In conclusion, Mr Chairman, I would remind this conference that we live in a country where there is nothing to stop a government pushing a Bill through Parliament within 48 hours, depriving a body of people of their right to British citizenship. There is nothing to stop a British government overruling a decision of the courts retrospectively, thus taking away a right already upheld by the law. Both of these have occurred in my time in the House of Commons. Statute law and case law are now, in my view, inadequate protection against the conditions that prevail in Britain today, and so there is now an overwhelming case for the introduction of a Bill of Rights to provide protection to the individual against abuses by the executive and administrative whims of government, by corporate bodies and by his fellow individuals. A Bill of Rights would frame formal, legal rights to which we would all be entitled. It should make the invasion of privacy a criminal offence, and the existing common and statute law should be interpreted in the light of its provisions. As well as privacy, it could deal with the collection and dissemination of information and the freedom of information, and it could therefore provide a framework against which the Lindop proposals could work.

A Bill of Rights in our modern conditions would not only be a powerful weapon for the protection of civil liberties and law reform. It would also be an educative instrument of great potential. Civil liberties in the United Kingdom are inevitably being eroded at an ever increasing rate. Urgent and decisive political decisions are required to make privacy more sacrosanct. This conference will contribute to that end. I wish you well in your deliberations and I have very much pleasure in formally declaring this important conference open.

Section 2

The Data Protection Committee Report

2.1. The Government Viewpoint
Lord Boston of Faversham,
Minister of State, The Home Office

First of all, I want to say that the Home Secretary is very sorry indeed not to be able to be here today. He has been detained on other pressing matters, and he sends his apologies. Also, he sends to the conference his very best wishes for the success of this important event and he wants to be kept fully informed about the outcome. Although you will miss his presence here, you will not miss what he would have said, because I shall be delivering the speech which he would himself have made.

From the Government's point of view, this conference could not be better timed. It is not always that events are well timed from the Government's point of view — you may have noticed! The conference comes at a most convenient moment in the Government's consideration of the Data

Protection Committee's report published last month. As an introduction to this session and to the conference generally I should like to explain the next steps the Government will be taking in response to this report and mention a few points on which the Home Secretary and his advisers will be particularly interested to hear your views.

The report raises questions with very wide implications for people in this country as the computer's capabilities and public perception of those capabilities spread rapidly wider and wider. This is an excellent subject for a wide-ranging and open debate here, and I am very grateful for the chance to take part in it.

Before explaining the next steps, I want to take this first public opportunity to thank you and the committee on behalf of the Home Secretary for all the work that you have done. I know that the committee set out to make their report a self-contained survey of the subject, and in that they have certainly succeeded. We are very grateful indeed to them for the time and effort put in.

I do not intend to dwell today on the history which leads us to consider Sir Norman Lindop's committee's report. It springs from the recognition of the problem by the Younger Committee on privacy in its report in 1972. They recognised that the handling of personal information on computers needed a separate and more thorough study than they could give it. In a White Paper on Computers and Privacy published at the end of 1975, to which David Steel has already referred, the Government announced their intention to set up the Data Protection Committee. Your report, is, of course, the result.

Technical developments since the White Paper, confirm that our concern for privacy in the age of the computer is amply justified. The machines are getting smaller and cheaper. Their applications are spreading wider. Once they were big, expensive, and reserved for specialist use by professionals who, under the guidance of the British Computer Society and other bodies, came to develop their own ethical standards. But the position is changing. The machines' capabilities are no longer a novelty. Their size and cheapness and their increasing sophistication, which makes them easier for laymen to use as tools of their everyday jobs, may mean that they are no longer being used by computer professionals alone. This has happened at a time when we are all perhaps a little less trusting of authority than we were.

But let us not be alarmist about this. There is one important general finding in the report we should keep in mind. The committee have conducted a most searching examination of this problem. They have found a few things to criticise. But it is worth emphasising that they have not found any significant evidence of abuse of information held by the Government, by other public agencies or by private sector bodies. That is worth remembering. But it is not an argument for necessarily leaving things as they are. There is, I think, a reasonable degree of agreement on the need for some safeguards for the confidentiality of personal information, and the generally favourable reaction to the committee's report, suggests we may be moving towards agreement on the nature of those safeguards.

Despite the comprehensive nature of the committee's report, there are some aspects, including costs, on which the committee could not give conclusive advice and which we must inquire into before formulating definitive proposals. I should like to explain how it is intended to do that. Our first task is to learn the views of those who would be affected by the report. The committee took evidence from a wide range of interested parties. We certainly do not intend to do the committee's job which they have done so ably and so fully all over again, but the nature and extent of the controls could have significant social and economic implications, and we must honour our commitment in the White Paper to consult those affected in devising our policy in the light of the report.

We intend to give all those affected a reasonable opportunity — but not a protracted one — to let us have their views. For that purpose the Home Office is arranging with all other Government departments to consult customers with an interest in computers and privacy. This will cover all those outside central Government departments, so it will include many represented here and industrial and commercial computer users, banks and credit institutions, various professions, particularly medicine, the police service, local authorities and local authority associations, as well as those having a more general interest such as indeed the NCCL itself, the British Computer Society, Justice, trade unions and so on. We shall also be consulting central government departments in their capacity as perhaps the biggest collectors and processors of personal information in the country. It will, of course, be open to others to offer their comments directly to the Home Office, where they will be carefully considered, and we shall be listening to the views expressed at conferences like this one and taking note too of the results of such surveys as the one the Institute of Data Processing Management has in hand.

There are several points the Government would like people to consider and on which we are looking for help from this conference. It is, we feel, absolutely vital to examine the committee's proposed scheme of control as an integrated whole as well as the details, and to look at it in relation to the purpose it is intended to serve and the actual or potential abuses it is intended to remedy or prevent. To do full justice to their work, we must begin by asking whether the scheme the committee have produced is right in principle. Is it directed to dealing with real and substantial problems? Will resources devoted to maintaining such a system of control be used to good effect? These are fundamental questions on which many of you have long ago formed your own considered views, but it is important that the answers should be reasoned through and not just taken for granted, which could be so easily the case.

Apart from these really fundamental questions, there are some others of considerable importance. I will deal with them under three headings. First, the structure and status of the Data Protection Authority; secondly, the scope of the authority's functions; and finally, what the proposed scheme of control will cost.

The committee have recommended for the Data Protection Authority a degree of independence from the Government which they recognise as unusual and for which they advance arguments of considerable force. I can well understand their view that the need to reassure the public about the proper use of personal information held by the Government, among others, can be met only by procedures which are independent of government. But without prejudice to the validity of that argument taken by itself, there are other considerations which the Government and I believe, Parliament must also have in mind. If the Data Protection Authority is to be independent of government to the extent that is proposed, by what other means is its accountability to be secured? It would be a very powerful body in its own field, with power to draw up and interpret codes of practice which it would be a criminal offence to breach; power to prosecute alleged offenders; power to investigate complaints and hold hearings. For its own functions it would need to maintain a system of records which could well contain extremely sensitive material. In large measure it would have power to determine the range of computer applications over which control needed to be exercised and the extent of the control required in each instance. Once it had established itself, its operations would be largely financed by charges levied on computer users. It would be a new member of that not too popular species, the Qango, and to those who are fearful of even the mildest members of that species it might well appear to have more than the usual number of teeth and claws.

As the committee pointed out, Parliament could, if it wished, reject a code of practice which the authority had presented, and could even request Her Majesty to dismiss any member of the authority who appeared to have become intoxicated with excess of power. But these would be extreme measures. The committee point also to the oversight that would be exercised by the Parliamentary Ombudsman and, in certain respects, by the Council on Tribunals. All I would say is that, before submitting to Parliament proposals for establishing an authority on the lines the committee recommended, the Government will need to be sure that there are adequate safeguards against such a body transforming itself into a self-regulating, self-expanding, bureaucratic empire. There may be ways in which the committee's proposed safeguards can be improved. If this conference has any suggestions to offer about this, I shall be very pleased indeed to consider them.

Another question I should particularly like to ask you to consider is where to fix the statutory limits of a Data Protection Authority's jurisdiction. Should all computerised personal information systems be covered? The committee recommend a degree of discretion over which applications other than those in central and local government should be made subject to codes of practice. But perhaps it is possible to identify in advance some applications which it would be unnecessary or too expensive in relation to the benefits, to subject to controls. On the other hand, there may be other applications which are so important that the authority should be compelled to subject them to controls. In considering how far to go, is the committee right in suggesting that the authority's ambit should extend to personal information systems of which part at least is automatic? Should they have gone further and brought in manual systems — something that David Steel touched on — or should they, on the other hand, have confined themselves to a more limited category of mainly or fully automatic systems? And if so, how should they be defined? Should the proposed controls recognise the practical difficulty and consequent expense which may be involved in applying controls to existing systems? Is there any way of minimising costs and practical inconvenience by allowing transitional periods or temporary exemptions for systems which cannot be modified and where compliance with the letter of the standards must await re-equipment with a new system? Could this be done in a way which did not leave loopholes in the effectiveness of the controls?

Finally, there is the financial aspect. The committee gave close attention to this in framing their recommendations, and it is crucial to their acceptability. Their assessment of the size and cost of a Data Protection Authority are necessarily heavily qualified, and the Government will have to make their own assessment. It is perhaps worth noting, for example, that the Swedish Data Inspection Board, serving a community of some eight and a quarter million, has a staff a little less than 30. The committee have estimated the cost of the Data Protection Authority, serving a community of some 55 million, on the basis that it would require a staff of 40. I am well aware of the limited value of this comparison. I mention the point simply to underline the importance of getting our cost estimate right.

It is, of course, much easier to argue against data protection on cost grounds than to argue for it. The benefits of data protection are intangible, but there are advantages in data protection, some of them recognised in the committee's report, which some cost-conscious critics might not think of. First of all, information can be a very valuable commodity indeed. Information collected at great expense could be of immense value to a competitor if he could steal it undetected. And conversely, deprivation of information by sabotage of a computer system or its records, could be very expensive. Then there is a growing public realisation of the capabilities of computers, and this could be felt in the form of resistance to their use or reluctance on the part of the public to co-operate in providing information where it is to be held on computers. The cost of data protection may be a reasonable price to pay for retaining the economies which computers can offer. Industrial efficiency and our international competitive position are not vague economic concepts; they mean jobs.

There is a respectable economic case to be made for data protection measures. We just have to be sure that we do not accept more restrictive and so more expensive controls than are necessary. We all know the economic maxim 'There are no free dinners'. The costs of data protection will fall inescapably on taxpayers and consumers as part of the price of goods and services provided by the public and private sector.

These are just some aspects of the report, I hope that the conference will be giving its attention to. There is just one final point I want to emphasise. The Government will certainly take into account views expressed on the report. But this period of consultation must not be allowed to go on for too long. It is in everyone's interest to limit the period of uncertainty.

This conference and the wider debate which we are not initiating will, I am sure, help the Government to reach sound decisions on the action to take in response to your committee's report. We look forward to hearing the outcome of your conference, and we wish the conference every possible success.

2.2   The Work of the Committee

Sir Norman Lindop, Chairman, Data Protection Committee.

As has been mentioned already, the origins of the committee lay in the White Paper of 1975, and that was in itself a follow-up, and some would say a rather belated follow-up, to the Younger Report of 1972. When the Younger Report was introduced to Parliament the then Home Secretary undertook to consult widely — a rather familiar phrase from the Home Office — and to prepare a statement, and there was then a gap of a number of years before that statement appeared in the form of the White Paper. The Home Secretary also undertook to institute for the first time, a review of the categories of personal information held by government computers. The point about the Younger Committee which makes the Data Protection Committee rather different was that the Younger Committee was precluded by its terms of reference from looking at the public sector. The Data Protection Committee, following the publication of the White Paper, had a wider remit.

At the same time as the White Paper itself was published, the Government published a very important supplement called *Computers — Safeguards for Privacy* which was in fact the implementation of the Home Secretary's earlier promise to review the categories of personal information held on government computers. It was given less attention that the White Paper itself, but we felt, on consideration, that it was a very important document, and we have recommended that it be brought up to date. In fact, an updated version of it is included as one of the appendices to our report, and we have recommended that it should be brought up to date annually. It does summarise the extent to which personal information is held on government computers and the extent to which transfers are authorised, either by Parliament or by administrative decision, between those files. This is part of the report to which we attach importance, and I mention it because it has not received much prominence in the past.

In fact, some of the points which have been mentioned by the Press almost as though they were emerging for the first time — and one or two of them were mentioned by David Steel this morning — have been enshrined in that document for the last five years: the fact that certain transfers of information take place, for example, from the Driver and Vehicle Licensing Centre to the police and the Inland Revenue, has been a fact since 1931. And the fact was given in the White Paper supplement of 1975 but seemed to have escaped people's notice. I think it illustrates the complexity of this subject and the temptation that there is to overlook significant details.

One of the cogent passages in the White Paper of 1975 said:

"The time has come when those who use computers to handle personal information, however responsible they are, can no longer remain the sole judges of whether their own systems adequately safeguard privacy."

The White Paper promised legislation setting out standards and criteria and establishing a permanent statutory agency, the Data Protection Authority. This is where we started from, because the Data Protection Committee was set up to advise the Government on the form the permanent machinery might take, and also to consider the objectives of the legislation.

The committee met 50 times in full session and several times in sub-committees and made a number of visits, and took precisely two years and a day to produce its report. We first met on 27 July 1976, and the final version of our report was delivered to the Home Secretary on 28 July 1978. Unfortunately, the Stationery Office strike intervened and the publication did not take place until December. And even that delay is to the members of the committee irritating, because we are aware of the pace of events, not only nationally, but internationally.

Most of us came to this task — and they are from very varied backgrounds — with no prior conceptions. One or two people were well versed in the whole issue; those two who will be speaking to you today, for example, came with a wide background in this area. But most of us had no prior specific connection with it and came into it with open minds, and from the early discussions it was clear that we were waiting to see what the evidence would bring. So we asked for evidence, and we certainly got it — by the trunkful. There is a very valuable summary of the evidence available in the conference papers today.

There was obviously a good deal of thought going on among responsible bodies and individuals, but one has to say that there was very little personal and public concern expressed either by individual members of the community at large or for that matter by the press. When we visited Sweden we were shown the press cutting file on data protection for two months, and it was thicker than the file in this country for two years. There was considerable difference from one society to the other in the attitudes on the whole question. And, as has been said earlier, we did not discover — and no-one else has produced evidence of — gross abuse in this area. That we did not discover it, is not necessarily conclusive evidence that it does not exist. We did not consider it our main job to carry out an investigative function searching for abuse. If we found any, we would certainly report it. But the fact that we did not produce any evidence and that others have not does not necessarily mean in this field that no abuse is taking place. In the nature of things it is sometimes impossible to determine until long afterwards whether or not an abuse has existed.

A good deal of the evidence was, one might say, predictable, but remember that we were taking evidence for the first time from both the public and the private sectors. There were those in the private sector who regarded the whole White Paper as what they called 'idealistic luxury' or as a concession to emotion and scaremongering by the media. There was no evidence of abuse, as I have said, no experience in this country of regulating such activities by legislation and, therefore, would it not be better approached by voluntary code — and in any case it would cost too much.

But those who opposed the whole concept were in a minority, and there was a significant majority — a considerable majority — with a pretty unanimous view that some form of legislation was necessary — as the White Paper has suggested — even in those areas where strong professional standards of conduct already existed; for example, in medicine or in statistics, where strong ethical codes already existed, the practitioners nevertheless felt the need of something in addition to that by way of a legislative framework. There was a general feeling among those who gave evidence to us — and remember, this was over two years ago — that there should not be undue delay.

Of course, there was anxiety about costs and the Minister has referred to this issue, that they might not be too high, on the one hand, or that they might be used as an excuse for doing nothing, on the other.

So we did a study — and I do draw attention to that study. One of the reasons for the bulk of the report is that we have included a good deal of information in the appendices arising from our studies. I think it is the first time that anyone has attempted such a survey. It is not in itself conclusive. It is not quantified very exactly. But, by hypothesising various types of control or regulative mechanism and by consulting a number of organisations that were good enough to help us, we got at least a view of the likely implications to a wide range of users. And we believe that, based on that survey, given a flexible régime such as the one we suggest, costs can be kept down. If they look very high there is something wrong, either with the privacy specification or with the existing present practice.

There will have to be compromise on costs, of course. This is part and parcel of the whole exercise of determining a compromise between the interests of the user, those of the data subject and those of the community as a whole.

In general, the government departments and public bodies from the public sector who have been questioned about this whole aspect for the first time, went along with the general view on the need for legislation, although with somewhat muted enthusiasm in some cases. It was because of this somewhat muted enthusiasm and also because of the scale of government and public body involvement with personal information that we attached importance to the degree of independence — constitutional independence — of the Data Protection Authority (DPA). We recognise that we are presenting ourselves with problems in making this proposal, but we felt it was important for the reassurance of the public. We mention in the report the dangers, to which the Minister has drawn attention, of setting up an independent bureaucracy, and we do try to hedge it about with as many

17

controls as possible. We do insist, of course, that Parliamentary control is paramount.

We concluded that it would be impracticable to set up a single, monolithic control mechanism; that the diversity of use and application, the many different relationships which exist between data subjects and users indicated that we must have some kind of flexible regime, and we were not inclined to favour many of the models which we had seen abroad. In the time which had elapsed since the Younger Report and the publication of the White Paper other countries had gone ahead. There were at least ten other countries in which legislation had either been enacted or was pending, and these are summarised in the Appendix to the report. But we felt that the British scene, with its balance between public and private sector, with the multifarious nature of users, with its international significance as part of the general international information exchange, required a flexible solution. There was also the point frequently made by users that everyone should be given time to adapt to a system when it was brought in. That was another reason for flexibility.

So we suggested the Codes of Practice approach, backed up by the force of, subject to approval by, Parliament, but each Code of Practice to be drawn up by consultation between the DPA and either individual or groups of users. We do attach importance to this consultative process; it is fundamental to the whole proposal.

Many of the arguments for a voluntary approach, which could be reflected in a Codes of Practice mechanism, would be stilled if it were established — as we believe it can be — that a regulatory approach based on codes of practice can be both relatively cheap and flexible. We have been attacked for restricting ourselves to computerised systems, but, as David Steel said, we were given a clear remit on this matter; we were asked to confine ourselves to automated systems. We chose to interpret that as widely as possible: that is, all those systems which had an element of automation in them. We realise that the same principles apply whatever methods are used to handle information, and we said so in the report. But we were clearly confined by our terms of reference. On the other hand, we did not feel — some of us — that this issue was quite as paramount as was made out, because we felt that the advance of technology was such, and the time scale was such, that the 100 per cent manual system dealing with a large amount of personal information was likely to disappear fairly soon, and that the proportion of automated information systems would constantly rise.

Mention has been made of the international context of the whole thing. I think this was one aspect of our work that many of us were unprepared for when we started, but which became ever more significant to us as we went along. It was one of the factors that persuaded many of us that there was more urgency in the situation than we had appreciated. As I have said, by July 1978, seven countries had legislated — Sweden, United States, West Germany, Canada, France, Norway and Denmark — and three more were on the verge of doing so — Austria, Belgium and Luxembourg. This does not exhaust the list of countries all over the world that are at an advanced stage of considering data protection legislation. The details of these legislations and proposals, as they existed last July, are contained in the report. It is immediately obvious that there is no uniformity between various countries about the way they approach this particular problem, but there is an unmistakable trend towards legislation and control. And if we are left behind, we believe we can suffer seriously commercially in this country. Trans-border data flows are now of such a volume, that compatible data protection regimes become essential. The Council of Europe, OECD, the EEC are all actively considering data protection and its international development. We believe it is important that the British view should be strongly represented, and we think that a British model would be important because we see drawbacks to many of the models which have been adopted elsewhere; not only as far as our society and our particular blend of interests is concerned, but also from the point of view of an international regime of control. We believe that the strength will be all the greater if the British contribution can be strong and based upon an agreed solution within our shores.

2.3 Practical Aspects of the DPC's Report

Charles Read, Director, Inter-Bank Research Organisation Member, Data Protection Committee.

What I want to do, is to look at the set of proposals and recommendations that we have made from a practical point of view and that I believe is pretty well the opposite of what David Steel was talking about. I do not believe he has done his homework, and I would ask him to follow Sir Norman's advice and read the report. If he had read it, I think he would not have said some of the things he said.

I believe that what we have put forward is extremely practical and I want to demonstrate why I think that is so and to point out some of the more important features of it. The fairness and the practicality of the whole thing results from trying to achieve the right degree of protection, and this can only be done, in my view, if you have a sound conceptual basis on which to formulate your detailed proposals — and I think we have. It can only be done if you have a very good appreciation of what is actually happening in the world of information handling, out there in the big wide world, and that consists not just of the small corners of the police force; the vast bulk of it is mundane, boring and uninteresting, and the vast majority of what goes on, goes on with the approval of all of us. We would not want to see it stopped. We would not want to see its cost raised. We would not want to see any ridiculous nuisances created in the functionings of various sectors of society. That is the bulk of what one is trying to legislate for, not just the little extremist case.

It is important to be practical and not to take extremist or political, polemical views. We tried to avoid such views and I think we succeeded. It is also necessary to take a realistic view of the way the information technology is developing, and I believe we have done that too. In addition, it is necessary for the legislation to be based on a realistic appreciation of the likely cost effects of the measures, and in particular to notice upon whom the cost might fall.

The other thing that is absolutely vital if it is going to be practical at all, is that it has to be robust, and robust in a situation which everyone would agree is fast changing.

Let me have a look at some of those points in turn, because there are some particular aspects of them that I should like to draw to your attention. Let me first deal with sound conceptual thinking, and here is the point at which I am at odds with Mr. Steel. Data protection in my view — and we have said so in the report — clearly does require the protection of the interests not only of the data subject, but also of the data user and also of the interest of society itself in seeing the information is handled to the benefit of society. Any view narrower than that, in my view, is both unworkable and foolish, and this concept of balance is absolutely vital to all that we have said. It is amplified even further if you take on board the notion, that we pointed out clearly in the report, that the interests even of the data subjects themselves are not limited to privacy. The best interest of the data subject often lies in the provision of data, and the provision by similar individuals in the same situation as himself — not in the withholding of it. There are many interests of individuals which are dear and cherished by all of us which have nothing to do with privacy and which need to be protected with equal enthusiasm.

It is also essential to recognise the very wide and changing variations in what is regarded as private, and especially to recognise that privateness is not an attribute of the data themselves. You have only to take a visit to Sweden, as some of us did, to see what is going on there. If you are a Swede and saw how very little privacy you had left, you would be interested in protecting it with a fair degree of viciousness. Fortunately, we are not in that situation here in this country. Fortunately, government files containing our income and Heaven knows what else are not freely available to the whole of society. And you may well reflect on whether you would like to see the whole of information handling moving in the Swedish direction, since that is the way to find yourself with remarkably little privacy and with the need strongly to try to cherish what little vestiges remain of it.

When data are regarded as private by a person, it is important to realise that he is not actually saying that he wants them to be known only to himself. What he is saying, is that he wants them to be known only to himself and to those others who he agrees should have them. The conditions under which that agreement is given are vital.

The agreement may not be given by himself. It may be given by others on his behalf, particularly by politicians in Parliament framing legislation on his behalf which will require that he will provide information about himself to various government agencies. The nature of the agreement, and the nature of the relationship between the data subject and those who want the data for a variety of purposes is an extremely important matter which we have dealt with extensively in the report. Sometimes that relationship is voluntary; sometimes it is contractual; sometimes it is at third hand and legislative. This relationship cannot be properly understood without looking at a number of particular aspects of the situation in which the agreement is reached or to which it refers.

The first thing that is important is the purpose for which the data are to be used. The second is the conditions under which they are to be applied to those purposes. The third thing is the conditions under which the agreement itself was reached in the first place. Fair terms for the provision of the data in the first place requires equal bargaining power and the ability to appreciate the other party's needs. That equality of power does not always exist, and certainly the ability to appreciate what exactly the other party wants it for, is all too lacking. Indeed, I am sure that if any of us think carefully about it, we find that our attitude is all the time ambivalent in all kinds of cases. Social workers are too efficient and nosey-parkerish; social workers should have stopped that baby being battered. The requirements conflict — you cannot have it both ways.

It is also vital to appreciate that in the use that is made of personal data the interests of the individual and the interests of society itself may conflict. Indeed, they almost inevitably conflict. There is a close parallel here in the concept of privacy and the concept of liberty. I have one thing in common with David Steel. I have also been reading John Stuart Mill, and if you have not recently read John Stuart Mill's essay on Liberty, I would commend you to do so. It gives a perfect statement of the whole concept of balance between the interests of individuals and the interests of society, and you can lift practically the whole thing from the concept of liberty to the concept of data protection. It is a question of balance, as Mill has pointed out, but it is not a question of a single point of balance. The balance between the interests of the individual and those of society on matters such as religious views or political views, clearly must weigh heavily in favour of the individual and against the interests of society. And at the other end of the spectrum, on matters of national security, the interests of the individual must be submerged or society cannot protect itself.

In between these two extremes there is a whole spectrum of points of balance. The difficulty is to find the correct point for each of the cases with which one has to deal.

Let me move on from the conceptual think bit to the thoughts about what is happening out there in the big wide world. I have already mentioned that the vast majority of what is going on in the handling of personal information, with or without technological assistance, is approved of, known about, mundane and uninteresting. And as you have been told several times already this morning, we did not find evidence of malevolence and abuse. This is the bulk of what we have to regulate.

But we have to look further than that. What will hapen in the future with regard to handling information? Roughly speaking, I think the answer to that with regard to conventional data processing — is a lot more of the same. It is going to extend into more firms, into more departments, into smaller scale operation. It will become easier and more wide-spread, but it will still be straightforward, mundane, boring and well understood, and, by and large, not abused.

There are, of course, cases where it is different, where things are being done that have not been done before because previously it was either technically impossible or not possible within the costs of the operation. Because the technology makes it now less difficult to do, or makes it more cost-viable, or makes it more realisable in a time scale such that the result is of value within a usable time scale, it is possible to develop something interesting, new and unique. But such cases are not largely in the area of straightforward, conventional data processing.

I would also point out that data protection should be concerned not merely with abuse, but also with over-enthusiastic bureaucracy and thoughtless efficiency. I should like to put that last phrase particularly in your minds — thoughtless efficiency, or the foolish seeking of the least cost solutions at all costs — at all human costs, that is. I believe that a lot of people at whom many of you might point the finger and say they are doing things that they ought not to do, would be horrified to be told that they were doing anything that was either naughty or disapproved of. What they are trying to do is the job they think they are asked to do as well as they possibly can, and they are not malevolent; they are either thoughtless, or they have been asked or instructed to pursue the wrong objectives.

Looking at the future of technology, to see what is happening beyond conventional data processing, we had first better have a quick look at conventional data processing itself. Roughly speaking, it is the general trend that everybody is fairly familiar with now — smaller, cheaper, less centralised, more distributed, more use of telecommunication transmission between particular modules of information handling. Also, in general, becoming easier to use and also, therefore, becoming no longer a tool for the elitist groups. It becomes increasingly possible for those who are unskilled in the technicalities of computing to use, and can leave the machines themselves in the hands of people with no better knowledge of the system than what one would expect from a normal secretary.

The result of those trends, in my opinion, is that the distinction between what is a computer-based system and what is a computer-assisted system and what is a solely manual system, is fading fast and will continue to fade even faster. You are coming up to the time when you will not be able to tell which is which.

Let us look at new uses, beyond conventional data processing. Full text retrieval techniques have been given special attention in the DPC report because they could impose a special threat and because they may prove difficult to control. A lot of the past views about methods of controlling data protection depend upon the ability to look at the content of the data held or the structure of the data held or the limitation in some way of what is being collected and used, as well as upon the definition of the purpose. In the case of full text retrieval systems, there is no limitation on the data; there are no semantic content constraints whatsoever; there are no significant structural constraints. You can put in whatever you like. It is not necessary to predetermine the data or the subject matter in order to design and implement the system. It is therefore not necessary to specify your purposes.

And, having put data into the system, you can search in a variety of ways; not merely a constrained, technical search. You can browse, you can fish, you can trawl through it. It is ideal for surveillance. This generates special problems of control. You cannot even infer the purposes to which the system is being put, and any form of regulation that is going to hinge itself on defining what data are and are not private, or are and are not private within certain purposes, is fraught and indeed I think it will fail.

Look now at word processing developments. This has something in common with full text retrieval in so far as here you have systems, the technicalities of which are concerned solely with the format of the information and the way in which it is sequenced. None of the technical software is in any way related to the semantic content of the information. But on anyone's definition, these are computer-based information handling systems. The information in them could certainly be personal. It is also very easy to use — only very minimal technical skill is required because the software can come to you fully packaged. These systems will become very widespread, in my view, and perhaps it is better to think of them as computer-assisted rather than computer-based systems, but, even on the narrowest definition, they will come within the ambit of control of automated systems.

The third new development that we have mentioned in the report is image processing — the processing of the digital representation of images; whether the images are of documents or maps or whatever is irrelevant. Conceptually this is completely indistinguishable from microfilm or any other form of photographic technique. It is merely that there is a substitute for paper, and again it is not concerned with the content of what is written upon the paper or the film or whatever it is. It is just another way of manipulating information.

Now I hope you can see why I for one believe that you not only will have immense trouble if you do not get away from tight definitions of what you do and do not mean by various kinds of equipment which should should not be regulated, but you also can see that you will in the end — in fact, in the fairly near future — be quite unable to tell one type of system from another. Since also, by the way, all systems are partially manual, there can be an interesting argument about whether the legislation should exclude the limiting case of systems which have no technical assistance, while all those which have varying degrees of technical assistance are included.

The legislative developments with which we are here concerned, therefore, need to be robust in the face of technical developments of this kind. And robustness means a number of things which I should like to enumerate. They must not be dependent on narrow definitions of computing. The indirect use of computers in assisting manual systems could, in fact, become the most widespread in its effects upon society. They must not be dependent on any definition of data, or data structure, or purposes, or the technical means for the handling. They must not attempt distinctions between technology-based and manual systems. There is no need, in my opinion, for an excited debate about the exclusion of manual systems. If you see the way that technology is moving — and you can fully expect a more widespread application of this new technology, if only on efficiency and cost grounds — you can see that it is really largely a waste of time, for it will not be too long before there will not be any manual systems of any size or significance, except those, by the way, that might be deliberately trying to avoid control — if control was limited in a silly way.

I would remind you once more, for those who have not read the document, that the DPC report does make clear that "the principles of data protection apply, no matter what methods are used". We have said so loudly and clearly, despite the limitation in terms of reference that we were given.

That leads me to a discussion to some degree of the principles. We have given our formulation of the principles — seven in total — which I do not propose to enumerate. I would like to ask you to note how they cover the three interest groups that are a vital part of the conceptual thinking — the data subject, the data user and society itself. And note how the concept of balance is embedded in that statement of principles.

We have not only enunciated the principles; we have gone on to say that when these principles are applied, the authority which will apply them will do this by reference to certain criteria; and we have enumerated seven criteria, which I shall not enumerate here. Here you see the manifestation of our recognition that none of the principles is applicable in the same degree in all cases. Therefore, they need to be applied case for case with an appropriate level of stringency. The criteria indicate what is relevant in determining the appropriate level of stringency, which once formulated throws quite a lot of light on to the means that might be judged sensible to achieve the appropriate level of stringency in each particular case. That also is an essential part of the thinking of our report.

The formulation of how the principles will apply to particular cases will be by means of codes of practice. These codes of practice are intended to be flexible and at the same time totally unambiguous and, given the interests of all concerned, the intention is to achieve that level of protection in a practical manner. We have thought quite a lot about this, and we have said that we think we can cover the bulk of the personal data handling in society by something like 50 codes of practice. It is not a very large number, and I do not believe they will be all that difficult to formulate. Indeed, I am convinced, by talking to people who are active in the business of information handling, that most major groups of users either already have written down or could with fair ease write down what would be a reasonable code in their own case. Thus, I think a lot of work will not fall to uninformed civil servants or others employed in the Data Protection Authority, but by the process of consultation, on which we have insisted, the work can be accomplished without that much difficulty.

There will be a need for modification from a standard code in certain instances where that can be justified, or — if you like — for tailoring it in some particular way in certain circumstances that might justify it, but I do not think that will be a very difficult problem either. And there will be some activities that are in a class of their own. These will be mostly in the public sector. For example, I believe one would need a unique code of practice for the DHSS system at Newcastle or the Hendon Police National Computer system. Although there is only one example of each case, a code could be written without any great difficulty.

The codes in some sense apply to classes of activities. There is no single criterion by which one can define the classes. Some activities group together by virtue of the professional activity concerned; the medical practitioners are an obvious case; solicitors another. A second criterion for classing is by the function performed — e.g. payroll, personnel records, current account banking, air line seat reservation. It follows that, for example, the code of practice for personnel records should not be in any way different in a government department than in a private organisation, and I would like to see that the same code is applied throughout society. If you classify in this manner by functions, common standards can be applied.

A third criterion relates to the characteristics of the hardware and software — i.e. the technical means used. The case of full text retrieval systems is an obvious example, and I believe that a very firm grip upon such systems must be taken whether they are being employed by government agencies or by private sector agencies. Surveillance is not something that is confined to snooping authorities. There is commercial surveillance which can be equally objectionable, and this kind of technology is very suitable for such purposes. So all who make use of certain techniques, no matter who they are, should I believe come under the same form and the same stringency of control.

Then there would be also certain special cases. Perhaps the obvious one here is computer bureaux, which are not in the same relationship as a straightforward data user. Nevertheless, they have responsibilities which should be clearly defined and regulated.

So you see another dimension of flexibility here in the grouping of things together from the point of view of devising codes of practice, which I believe is not merely desirable, but inescapable.

The major advantage of formulating codes of practice is I believe that they provide the means of applying those principles which are applicable in a given case, and of specifying the degree to which they are applicable. This involves the recognition that there are many cases in which some parts of what has been held by some people to be a universal requirement, simply are not applicable. For example, that data should be disposed of or destroyed the moment they are no longer required for the purposes for which they were provided. If we apply that just in that simplistic manner, that means there will be no archives whatever; there will be no records for future historians whatsoever. And that is an absolute nonsense. There would be no data available for medical research, for example, by statistical medical data banks — another nonsense. You cannot apply such an elementary statement of principle universally and be sensible about it.

The same is true about the so-called right of access. If there is a right of access universally applied, it will completely up-end the possibility of various systems existing at all. For example, in the case of statistical research in medicine, where large data banks of information about individuals are used to try to discover new diagnostic formulations of one kind or another, it would be a nonsense if we could all make a nuisance of ourselves by asking what data they hold about us. It never emerges in an identifiable way. It is never used for the clinical treatment of the individuals concerned. It only ever emerges as groups of numbers of one kind and another. Provided there is sufficient control of who has access to that raw material and what forms of output emerge from it, I for one would put my head on the block and say: no right of access — that is simply disruptive, stupid and unnecessary. The safeguards can be achieved by another method, and that is how they should be achieved.

So there is a variation in the applicability of the various means of protection as well as the degree to which the various principles apply, and not to recognise this would lead to what I believe would be a totally impractical approach.

The second advantage of code of practice approach is that it does provide the opportunity for the involvement of users, which is vital — as Sir Norman has already mentioned. It also provides opportunity for the Data Protection Authority itself to become what we would like it to become a friendly body — one that is co-operating, one that is trying its best to understand what are the real requirements, not only of the data subjects but of the users and of society itself.

The third advantage is that it would make it fairly easy to amend the requirements in given cases, given technical changes of one kind or another, given shifts in the activity patterns of the people being regulated by the code. So it gives a further degree of flexibility of that kind.

Fourthly — and very importantly — it enables this particular form of regulation to embrace any already existing codes of practice. For example, the medical profession, among others, has excellent ethical codes which prescribe in considerable detail exactly what information may be held by whom and to whom it may be passed and under what conditions. They even have extensive professional sanctions to back them up. So have psychiatrists, and so have many others, although there are all too many others who do not. Such existing practices could be embraced and reinforced by the new codes of practice, and this we know would be welcomed by the bulk of the people with whom we have discussed the matter.

It also is true that in many cases there are operational guidelines of one kind and another which concern themselves with the technical means of safeguarding the security of information and so on, often well formulated, well enforced. They too, can be hauled on board and embraced and given now the force of law.

It also enables one to straddle and bring together any other legislative requirements which may already exist for particular data users — and there are many of these. You will find in the report a particular example from the area in banking, and you will see in one of the appendices a long list of all the pieces of legislation which currently are on the Statute Book requiring the banks to disclose personal data to a whole lot of different bodies. Those too must be straddled and embraced by the code of practice, so that there we have a consistent and total statement of exactly what the requirements are in the particular instance.

Fifthly, there are many large organisations handling large amounts of personal data for a whole lot of different purposes. It would be impractical, I believe, to devise rules applying to all of their activities taken together. It will be much easier to break it into the modules called codes of practice. Thus, the code of practice about the payroll will tell them what to do with that. The code of practice about personnel records will tell them what to do with that. The code of practice with regard to their debtors' ledger will tell them what to do with that. and so on. That will be easier for them to comply with and understand. It will be simpler for the DPA to formulate. And, in addition, it has the enormous merit that the same code would be applicable in all of the different industries where the same function is being performed. This will lead to a consistent and logical formulation across the whole spectrum of society, which I believe is highly desirable.

Lastly — and perhaps not quite so important — this modular approach to the matter will allow the DPA to phase its work. It will have to phase its work, of course, since it cannot pick up the whole spectrum of data handling and legislate for the lot all at once. It simply would not be possible.

If you look at all this in the light of our findings on the subject of costs, you will find that the cost study reinforces this approach. It led us to see that any over-rigid, over-simplified, approach of applying principles in a simplistic and non-differentiated manner leads to either ridiculous costs or inappropriate levels of control, or totally unnecessary procedures, even to the serious hindrance of the functioning of the organisation itself, none of which is what the individuals would wish to happen. It can even in some cases lead to the total impossibility to comply with the reulatory requirement. Nothing could be more foolish than producing rules that cannot reasonably be complied with.

This flexible and practical approach that we have put forward I believe meets the requirement for a reasonable level of protection and it can do so at moderate cost, provided you involve those who know about each particular operation, and who can take a proper account of all the relationships and interests involved.

The relationship between data subjects and data users is very important and varies very widely. Sometimes it is direct and straightforward. For example, we all have such a relationship with the Electricity Board. Sometimes it is rather indirect, such as in the case of mail order companies serving their customers through agents. And sometimes it is very ephemeral; often of very short duration. Each airline has data about me every time I fly. But what do they know? They know my name, and that might be false if I choose to give them that. They might know about my dietary requirements, and they know from which airport I am to leave and where I propose to arrive. And that is all. I do not believe that I should be given the right of access to that data about myself in those files, provided they do not disclose it to anyone else without my knowing what they are doing with it, provided they safeguard access to it in a sensible manner, and so on. It is a nonsense for such an ephemeral relationship to be treated in the same way as a more serious relationship. And there are many other examples which I am sure you can think of for yourselves.

Other merits of the flexible approach which I should like to point out are these. If you take a flexible approach of this kind, there is no need for exemptions. And I regard that as of very great importance indeed. Of course there will be some exemptions on the very fringes — the matters concerned with national security clearly require exemption. If they were not so exempted, there could be no national security. It would be foolish to argue otherwise. But in all other cases there is no need for exemption. If one can correctly formulate the right level of control at reasonable cost and in a practical manner, why would any activity want to be exempted? Nearly all of the arguments for exemption are related to impracticability or high cost, or inappropriateness of the control.

Secondly, it does allow an appropriate choice of the right level of bureaucratic inefficiency — and that is one of the best safeguards I know of the interest of individuals. I was very sad to see that an earlier speaker this morning had evidently not read what we had to say in our report on the subject of national identification numbers — we have said firmly and clearly that we do not like them, and we have said why. What we are saying — and I repeat the phrase — is that we would like to commend the choice of a certain measure of *bureaucratic inefficiency* in order to safeguard privacy, liberty and other cherished human values. I think it is a rather nice and essentially British idea — the deliberate engineering of bureaucratic inefficiency. It appeals to me enormously, and just because the others in countries abroad have not thought of it, I do not think it is wrong!

2.4 Legislating for Data Protection

Paul Sieghart, Barrister, Member Data Protection Committee

Charles Read put his finger on it when he said that what all this is about is finding the right point of balance. Indeed, I think that was perhaps fairly obvious from our two first contributors. David Steel was speaking very much from the point of view of the individual citizen, and the Minister, not surprisingly, was speaking very much from the point of view of the organisation of those private citizens into groups that need to be administered, governed and all the rest of it. Whether it is in the public sector or the private sector makes no difference at all.

Of course, it is precisely because there is a different perception when you are a private citizen being administered from when you are an administrator administering private citizens, that long before Plato and Aristotle there has always been some degree of tension between the individual and the group, the citizen and the state, the employee and the company that employs him, and so on. And it is those tensions which are the meat of politics and of political science and of a good deal of philosophy.

All of which is extremely interesting in the abstract. In the course of what I suppose is now getting on for fifteen years that I have been tussling with these problems myself, I confess I have learned a great deal, starting off— as one is bound to when one first comes into this kind of thing — with what you might call the David Steel view of the individual alone, and then beginning to see how that individual also calls at the same time for electricity supply, getting the right gas bill and not the wrong one, wanting to make sure that his bank manager, when he gives a reference about him, does not confuse him with the other Joe Bloggs and has not missed the fact that he did in fact pay £600 into his bank account the day before yesterday — in fact, the ordinary citizen also demands that he is properly administered. Therefore, we are all, I think a little schizophrenic about these things, and it did not take us very long on the Data Protection

Committee to realise that the principal reason why we were there at all was because there are balances to be struck between different desires, different requirements, different interests — all of people, but of people wearing different hats, sitting on different chairs and doing different jobs.

I am afraid I am one of those who, rather like the late and unlamented Reichsmarschall Goering, reaches for my revolver when I hear abstractions like 'the state', 'society', 'the pound' and all the rest of it. Quite horrible things have been done in history in support of abstractions of that kind. None of those things exists. It is all about people, and it is all about individuals. And that faceless civil servant who is administering you from some distant desk — in fact, he too is a human being. He too is fallible. He too is inclined at times to be arrogant, at times to be over-zealous — like all the rest of us! What we have to try to achieve is some kind of a system where the right balances are struck.

But now comes the most interesting question, of course. Who is going to strike those balances? And how is he going to go about it? That is really the subject matter of Part 3 of the report, and if I may commend to those particularly who are concerned with civil liberties and Qangos and the dangers of giving too much power to too few people, I commend that part particularly. That was a subject with which we had to wrestle on the Data Protection Committee, and it took us quite a long time, not to resolve disagreements between us, but to try to find once again a balance of trying to ensure so far as possible, that the scheme which we were devising and advising the Government on would be practical, would work and would avoid all the foreseeable dangers about these things.

Let me first explain how the problem comes about. If you do have a conflict of interests and you have to adjust different interests in order to strike the right balance, somebody has got to do that. And it is elementary, not only to every lawyer, but to any citizen who has got any sense of fairmindedness, that the person who does that has got to be independent of the other two. Let me emphasise that the question in practice will probably only arise in a tiny minority of cases. The overwhelming bulk of the information handling, automated or manual, which goes on today and which is going to go on more and more automated and less and less manual in fifty years time, is going to be entirely innocuous, consensual, and will meet the interests of all parties concerned because in fact they have common interests.

Looking as we did, and as we reported in Part 2 of the report, at the information handling in various sectors of the community that actually go on today, the overwhelming majority of cases are cases where the interests of the data subject and the interests of the data user are precisely the same. For example, data subjects and their bankers have exactly the same interest in keeping the financial information about the running of the customer's account confidential between the data subject and the banker. Put yourself in the position of a banker. How long would you stay in business if you had a leaky information system as a result of which outsiders started getting information about your customers' accounts? In no time at all your customers would leave you in droves. You would shut up shop, and the High Street bank across the road that had the better system would get them all.

The same applies to the Electricity Board, which has exactly the same interest in sending you the correct bill so that you will pay it on the nail and not query it, as you have in getting the correct bill. It is only in a comparatively small number of cases that you will find that there is a conflict of interests. That is obviously the small number of cases on which attention concentrates, not only in the media, but also — rightly — in government, and — rightly — in some of the workshop discussions that we shall be having at this conference.

What one needs to look at is, where there is going to be such a conflict of interest, who is going to resolve it? The first principle is that it has got to be resolved by someone who is independent of all the parties concerned.

We have plenty of experience in this country of setting up courts, arbitrators, tribunals, Qangos of every kind, to do that kind of thing between different interest groups. We have very little experience in doing it where one of the interest groups happens to be a government department. It is, as it happens, one of the problems which we have met increasingly in the last twenty years or so, that we are rather short of experience in what continental countries would call administrative law, administrative courts, and all that kind of thing. Perhaps the first model that we have developed was the introduction of the Parliamentary Commissioner for Administration, better known as the Ombudsman.

When we started to think who should be this arbitrator, this independent third party that should mediate and ultimately arbitrate between conflicting interests, we looked at any number of possible models. The first thing that became plain was that in all those other countries where there was data protection legislation, either passed or going through their respective parliaments, where they had the system of a data protection commissioner or a data protection authority or some independent body of that kind, they placed enormous importance on the independence of that body, both from the individual data subjects and from the users. The reason for that, of course, is obvious.

But, of course, one of the major users of information handling, automated and manual, in this and in any other country is not only central government, but also local government. There are many public sector bodies which are not technically part of government, and yet which the citizen perceives as part of the government machine: as, for example, the police, which is not part of the government machine at all, but a series of local forces; the National Health Service, which is an independent entity and, oddly enough, does not come under the absolute direction of the DHSS although very few people know that.

What kind of a body do you set up which is going to be independent of everybody? Then you have to start looking at what you mean by "independent", and when you start considering that, you look at something like the Independent Broadcasting Authority. The Independent Broadcasting Authority was set up — or rather, the Independent Television Authority as it then was — with great fanfares that it was going to be the *independent* television authority, as if the BBC were not the first model of an independent broadcasting authority anywhere in the world. That, of course meant independent of the BBC — not necessarily quite as independent of the programme contractors, and so on. And you really have to ask yourself: 'Independent of whom, and independent in what respects?' How, for example, could, in the worst imaginable case, central government bring pressure to bear on an independent data protection authority?

What one then has to do — and we did it — is to say to oneself: 'All right. We will role-play the Secretary of State of the future' — none of the present or past ones —'with horns and cloven hooves, whose one concern is to dominate the Data Protection Authority. What can he do?' Exercise no. 1 is to appoint all his cronies. Exercise no. 2 is to dismiss the ones that do not fall into line. Exercise no. 3 is to make sure they do not get paid enough or they do not get their pensions. Exercise no. 4 is to give them directions about how to conduct their affairs and what to put into the codes of practice if there is an element of dispute or something of that kind. And if all that fails, what other things can one think of?

We went through all those, and what we have tried to do, bit by bit, detail by detail, is to create a scheme under which I do not suppose it would be impossible, but it would be exceedingly difficult and certainly very visible, if anybody tried to do any of those things. Take, for example, appointment and dismissal of the members of the Data Protection Authority. Under the English constitutional system nobody can be appointed to anything unless somebody appoints them. So you look to see who is there who can actually appoint people to public positions. It is no good saying 'the Government' in a situation of that kind. What is left? It so happens that there is a very convenient constitutional precedent — the Crown by letters patent. This is an appointment on the recommendation of the Prime Minister and not of a particular Secretary of State. That is the best that we can do when it gets to appointment.

But you can do rather better than that for removal. There are precedents for saying that some people — for example, High Court judges — hold office for life and they cannot be removed at all except, in effect, by an Act of Parliament. We considered that, and we came to the conclusion that for life might be a bit long, because you would have rather a gerontocratic Data Protection Authority after several years. So we said for a fixed period, during which they cannot be removed except, in effect, by Act of Parliament.

How long should the fixed period be? If you think for a moment, provided it is almost certain to extend over at least one general election, there is a reasonable prospect that the political parties will rapidly realise that if either of them packs in while it is in power, the other one will do the same next time round. So with any luck, they will be left alone and the members of the DPA will be appointed on merit, and therefore we said five years. And there is a great deal of that kind of thinking which runs through that part of the report.

Having achieved — we like to think — the highest degree of independence which is practical in the English constitutional system, we then immediately came up against the problem which the Minister very rightly pointed out: if you have a body which is going to be very independent, you immediately run the risk that that body is going to become — in his own words 'self-regulating, self-expanding and ultimately arbitrary and irresponsible'.

So, having made them independent, how do you then make them accountable and for what and to whom? We propose that they should be made as accountable as it is possible within our political system to as many other bodies and institutions as we could find on the English constitutional map. First of all, the Data Protection Authority must itself obey the law, and in particular, must not exceed the powers that it is given by the Data Protection Act. The proper independent institution to police and regulate that, is the courts. So anybody can take the Data Protection Authority to the courts, and if the Data Protection Authority is found not to have done its legal duties or not to have done them properly, the court will say so and it will overrule it. So that is one major constraint and a very necessary one on any authority which is going to have powers.

The second one is the Council on Tribunals. The Data Protection Authority will to some extent have an adjudicatory function a little bit like some of the administrative tribunals which proliferate in the country. The Council on Tribunals is there in order to ensure that anybody who has any adjudicative function goes through all the proper procedures, observes natural justice, gives everybody an opportunity of having his say, and so on and so on. So, in exercising that function, the DPA will be accountable in effect to the Council on Tribunals.

Then there is a very large grey area of administrators who are given powers by Parliament fairly widely defined, within which they can exercise a certain amount of discretion. How does the citizen test whether that discretion has been fairly and properly exercised? Until the institution of the Ombudsman in this country, there was no way at all. If Parliament gave a power to an administrator which was not circumscribed and he was not told how to exercise it, there was no way in which the courts or anybody else could ever say that he had maladministered. The Ombudsman system has the great merit that the Ombudsman can look at any file of any government department and report to Parliament and decide whether there has been a maladministration. Not a breach of the law; not abusing power or going beyond the power that was given by the law; simply coming to the wrong decision, maybe by the wrong procedure.

Therefore, we have proposed that the Data Protection Authority be subject also to the jurisdiction of the Ombudsman. But the Ombudsman, according to the Parliamentary Commissioner Act, is only allowed to look at the administration of government departments. And the DPA is not to be a government department. On the contrary, it is to be independent of government. How can one get the Parliamentary Commissioner to be able to look at the DPA without making the DPA a government department We sought advice on this subject and we were presented with a perfectly brilliant solution by one of the ex-Ombudsmen. He said: 'Very simple. In the Data Protection Act you set up a special Parliamentary Commissioner only to do the Ombudsman's work for the DPA. Then you appoint exactly the same chap who is already the Ombudsman to do that!'

But, of course, the most important channel of accountability ultimately can only be to Parliament, and it is in that respect that we were very glad to find that the Ombudsman provided a very good model for our proposal. You see, when the Ombudsman was first created in this country, exactly the same problem arose. If he was going to invigilate what went on in government departments, obviously he must be as independent as possible of government. Therefore, he reports directly to Parliament, and his accountability is direct to Parliament. Parliament has set up — as I hope it will in the case of the DPA — a special Select Committee which has the responsibility of being the body to whom the Parliamentary Commissioner reports and is accountable. Precisely the same thing we would like to see and we have recommended in the case of the DPA.

It is perfectly true that there is one distinction between the DPA and the Ombudsman. The Ombudsman has no regulatory power; he can only report. He cannot actually make regulations and he cannot actually make people do things. The DPA will have some powers, and indeed the Minister listed several of them. I was interested to hear from him that one of the powers which apparently he and his department are worried about, is that the DPA will have the power to prosecute people who infringe the codes of practice. But every single one of us in this room has the right to prosecute anybody for any criminal offence. In this country there is still, although it is not often exercised, an absolute right of private prosecution on the part of anyone.

But it is true that the DPA will have some powers, including what is technically a legislative power, because, if the codes of practice are going to work and are going to have teeth, obviously they must have the force of law. It would be quite wrong for the DPA to make laws of its own without consulting anybody else. Only Parliament can make laws in this country. Therefore, our proposal was that when the DPA has worked out a code of practice, in consultation with users, data subjects and everyone else concerned, the Authority will propose to Parliament the code of practice which it thinks ought to regulate that particular area of data processing. And Parliament can then say whether it likes it or not. If Parliament likes it, it will pass it into law; and if Parliament does not like it, it will not — it will throw it out. And if it throws it out, the DPA will have to go back to the drawing board and start again.

Let me emphasise again that there is only likely to be a difference of opinion in a few very rare cases. In the overwhelming majority of cases there is going to be no problem at all. For example, take the case of the airline reservation system. I cannot conceive that there can be any real argument about what ought to go into a code of practice for airline reservation systems. Charles Read rightly said that he does not mind in the least airlines having that amount of information about him in order to get him on the right aeroplane at the right time. And he added, 'provided, of course, they do not give that information to anybody else'. Most airlines do not want to give that information to anybody else. They have not the slightest interest in that, and therefore, no doubt, the code of practice will say, 'And when you have finished with those data, ultimately you will scrub them, and meanwhile you will not give them to anybody else'. Nobody is going to disagree about that.

I can quite see, if one wanted to construct a situation fraught with danger, that if an airline thought there was some advantage in giving to some Arab government a computer print-out of all its passengers who order Kosher meals and whose tickets are being paid for by substantial public companies, in order that those Arab governments can then put those companies on the Black List, yes indeed, there would be a public scandal about that. Therefore, the Code of Practice obviously would have to prevent that kind of thing from happening. But I cannot conceive that any airline — at all events in this country — would object to having a provision saying 'you do not pass that information outside the airlines'.

As I have said, in the great majority of cases you will have no conflict of any kind. Let us now take one of the rare cases where there really is a conflict. I suspect that, as in most cases, if you get the practitioners who are really interested in the nuts and bolts sitting round the same table, you will find that the area of disagreement will very rapidly narrow. But let us assume that even that has not happened. The next thing that we propose is that there should be a public hearing. Let the DPA organise a hearing open to the public where everybody who has got any concern in this question can come and argue it out. And let us see whether at the end of that it is not possible to find a constructive solution.

But again — and we are now down to about one case in a thousand, or even fewer — let us assume that the conflict persists and appears to be incapable of resolution. Then ultimately, if the parties concerned simply cannot agree at all, there is only one body in this country that can sort it out, and that is Parliament. Therefore, every Code of Practice has to go to Parliament, and if the DPA puts up a Code of Practice which is still being objected to, after all those procedures, by one or other of the parties that is going to be concerned by its operation, parliament will debate that, and Parliament will decide. And if it so happens that one of those parties is central government, then central government will have to persuade Parliament that it is right about that particular issue and that the Data Protection Authority is wrong. And if Parliament so decides, that ought to be the end of the matter, at all events until the next general election.

That is, in very summarised and simplified form, the conclusion that we have come to in this particular part of our report. We think that, from a practical point of view, it is feasible, workable and will not only protect everyone concerned — the data subject, the users against silly high costs, society at large, which derives great benefits from the right flows of the fight information to and from the right people — but that, without being in any way a constitutional innovation, it will also command the confidence of everybody concerned, including the public at large.

I am particularly concerned about one matter. We did say in our report that we quite saw that this solution might not immediately appear acceptable to everyone, and I was not, of course, the least surprised to hear from the Minister that the Home Office has at least some doubts about this system. We did say that one of the ways in which problems of this kind have been dealt with in this country in the past has been ultimately to put these matters under a Minister and to make a Minister responsible, on the theory which we still have of Ministerial accountability to Parliament. But, we explained that, while we very much considered the possibility of a Minister ultimately having the deciding voice, we unanimously came out against that. We set out what we thought would be the necessary safeguards if a Minister had any say in the matter at all, but we then went on to say that, even with those safeguards, we still thought it was much better that the Minister should keep out of it altogether and that the DPA should be, rather like the Ombudsman, directly accountable to Parliament.

Can I just end by echoing what I think everybody, without any difference, has said. I hope that it will not be too much longer before Parliament is actually invited by the Government to voice its views on this; that a Bill will be presented before too much longer. It is more than high time. We have now been looking at this subject for a great many years. Every other industrialised and civilised country in the world is legislating hard. If we are the last to do it, we may have the advantage of the best Data Protection Act because we will have gained from the experience of other countries, but we may suffer considerable disadvantages in other respects.

2.5   Data Banks, Past and Present

Joe Jacob, Lecturer in Law, London School of Economics.

The NCCL was the first British organisation to arouse public concern about what became known as the Data Bank Society.

It began its concern with the issue in 1968 by publishing *Privacy Under Attack.*This was a comprehensive description of the various ways in which privacy was (and still is) in danger. As the campaign proceeded it focused on these issues: (1) unreasonable privacy invasion by the media; (2) the activities of private detectives; and (3) the use of banks of data relating to individuals held in the private, but more particularly the public sector.

The NCCL can claim only a small part of the credit for the establishment of the Younger Committee on Privacy. Perhaps the most important result of that inquiry (apart from further inquiries) was the introduction of a new code on privacy by the Press Council. It can claim more credit for the exposure of the methods of some unscrupulous private detectives which resulted in the case of *DPP v Withers.* This, however, is not the place to discuss either the Press Council's Code or the current state of the law as it has been left by the decision in *Withers* and the Criminal Law Act 1977.

By the time the House of Commons debate on the 1970 Privacy Bill, the NCCL had already seen that the most important questions were not simply privacy invasion in the private sector. On the contrary, the most important issue was the handling of the vast information stores in the public sector. The NCCL was probably responsible for the grievous, but then understandable mistake, of thinking that this issue was linked to the probable impact of computers. At that time others were falling into the same error. So also the NCCL and others fell into the trap of associating this issue with privacy questions.

However, unlike many others involved in the field, the NCCL quickly recognised these conceptual mistakes. It co-sponsored the 1970 Conference on the Data Bank Society and it rapidly followed that event with the drafting of the Control of Personal Information Bill. As will be seen some eight years later, the Data Protection Committee (DPC) has largely come to the same conclusions.

Among the elements of the CPI Bill was the establishment of a flexible basis of control of data banks of all types in both the public sector and the private sector. This is what the DPC is asking for. The NCCL in 1970 and the Data Protection Committee in 1978, both recognised that although there must be a common core to the basis of control, significant variations as to, for example, the rights of access by data subjects to the stored information, are necessary according to the functions and utility of the data bank. Whereas the NCCL in 1970 said this should be done by the imposition of conditions in a license, the DPC now says it should be done by registration and the application of Codes of Practice. The difference is not unimportant but nor is it fundamental.

There are three respects in which the NCCL original proposals differ from Lindop's. First, the NCCL suggested a rigid divide between the "licensing body" (which it calls the Data Bank Tribunal) and the investigating machinery. Lindop has modelled his overseeing authority on the Health and Safety Executive and correspondingly followed that pattern with his investigation machinery. Again the difference is not fundamental, but it appears that if an overseeing body has the direct power to put organisations out of business, then it should be separate and be seen to be separate from the machinery of investigation which leads to that event.

Secondly, the NCCL was concerned to create a range of civil remedies suited to the new mischief. The DPC (which devotes but one page to the question) appears hopelessly inadequate. The CPI Bill of 1970 created injunctive powers to order erasure etc. of information and to order persons wrongly informed about a data subject to be correctly informed. In addition it created not merely a right to damages but also it sought to set out the basis on which a court of law might assess the amount.

Thirdly, the NCCL Bill applied to conventional as well as computerised data banks. However, instead of applying the controls to data banks of any size, the NCCL limited the regulation to data banks on over 100,000 individuals. The reason for this was not simply a desire to exempt small scale operations, so saving bureaucratic developments. It was more fundamentally that the issue was seen as a significant feature of the problems that individuals have when faced with the large bureaucracies of our age. It was for that reason also that the NCCL proposals avoided the question of whether a data bank was computerised.

All in all the similarities between the 1970 CPI Bill and the DPC recommendations are too striking to pass without comment. What is more significant is the failure of successive governments and Home Secretaries to respond or even to demonstrate that the questions are understood. So far the only legislative changes that have been made are some minor reforms as regards credit reporting and spent criminal records. One is perhaps left wondering not what is to be done about this issue, but rather more why British governments are so uninterested in the state of liberty in Britain.

2.6   Report from the Workshop on the Data Protection Committee Report

Jo Kenny, British Computer Society.

The easiest way for me to summarise the whole workshop is to say that at the end of the day there was widespread acceptance and support for the Data Protection Committee Report. We had a lot of discussion in detail, but there was no general feeling that the recommendations should not go ahead, no general feeling that they were in principle unworkable, unrealistic or incorrect. There was, however, quite a lot of discussion and some dissension.

We had an advantage that we had in the workshop the chairman of the DPC and two of the members. Therefore, many of the comments that were made were immediately fielded by one of the three committee members there. What became apparent to me was that, even where the report had been read, there was still a great deal of difficulty being met in detailed appreciation and understanding. That was not because of any fault in the way the report was written, but the problems of actually absorbing what was being said.

Rory Johnston, a computer journalist, suggested to the workshop that the proposed legislation could fail completely to control computer users who are determined to contravene them. Large computer systems are so complex that it would be quite impractical for Data Protection Authority inspectors to try to probe and understand them without the owners' willing co-operation. Existing laws, such as defamation, are a better framework for protecting the public than new administrative machinery.

Having said that at the end there was widespread support, there was, of course, a lot of discussion, and I will just mention the four or five areas in which discussion was concentrated, because, if one accepts the report in general, discussion comes down to the actual measures suggested: the statutory principles put forward for a Data Protection Authority to follow; the statutory criteria, which is how these principles should be interpreted — both of which are in general terms; the guidelines for the Codes of Practice.

It was stated by Sir Norman Lindop that it was accepted by the committee that, in establishing a Code of Practice, there would be widespread public debate. It would not be done in isolation. That dealt with a lot of the questions that had arisen in discussion.

It was suggested that users cannot be sure what precisely will be involved in complying with the new law until the Codes of Practice are drafted, although some existing Codes (e.g. on government statistical application or psychiatrists' records) might form a practical basis for the DPA's work in those fields.

We had a lot of talk about the question of computer-based records and manual-based records with a widespread feeling amongst quite a number in the workshop that the recommendations should also apply to manual records. The final conclusion was that it might be difficult in practical terms to do this, even though this comment came from people who would like to see the recommendations extended to manual records, but that if a code of practice was established for a particular application, this could probably be extended to apply both to manual records eventually as well as to records based on some automatic process.

We also spent a lot of time on the question of collection of data: should data handling include controls on the collection? Should people be told at the point of collection exactly what the purpose was for which the data were being collected? This became of particular significance because of the question of trans-national data flow — data going over borders. This is a subject which is now causing a lot of widespread debate, and it was agreed by the workshop as a whole that controls would need to include controls on the collection of data as well as just the handling of data, the reason being that if data is collected in one country and processed in another, it will be going across a border and just controlling the processing by itself in any one country may be insufficient.

At the end of the day there was widespread support and acceptance that controls of this type were going to appear anyway. There was an international movement for such controls, and the most realistic thing to do was to get an authority established, get it working, and concentrate effort on the Codes of Practice.

2.7 Report from the Workshop on the Costs of Privacy Legislation

Edward G. Cluff,
Institute of Data Processing Management

This workshop recognised that the DPC report clearly understood the need to keep costs of privacy legislation to a minimum, as evidenced by one comment in the report that one particular choice, had it been made, would have confirmed the fears of those who thought that the recommendations would be the occasion for a major extension to bureaucracy. Nevertheless, it is clear that the extent of the major part of the costs falling on the user cannot be quantified until each relevant code of practice has been agreed. There was one strongly expressed view that the cost of running the DPA may have been underestimated, both in terms of the salaries necessary to attract the right staff and the number of applications involving personal data.

There was a recognition, however, that the direction taken by the DPC, which has satisfied the representatives of some of the professional computing organisations, will make a major contribution to minimising the costs by making the legislation more manageable. For example, identification of the user departments and their applications as the subjects of control, rather than the computer department and its files. The DPC have clearly recognised the difference between the protection of data or its security and the questions of privacy. This recognition helps to place the responsibility where it can be controlled, as distinct from legislation in some countries which has not been able to distinguish between the two.

There was also a welcome for the concept of a hierarchy of security measures which would relate the measures to the need. There was a suggestion that we would do well also to differentiate between security, which seeks to prevent unauthorised access, and confidentiality, which seeks to prevent the abuse of authorised access.

The workshop also noted the preference of the DPC for registration instead of licensing, which also tends to minimise costs.

The workshop welcomed the manner in which the DPC had tried to encourage the Government to broaden its legislation to encompass non-automatic systems in spite of its terms of reference. There was a strong feeling that it is essential to cover manual systems.

Apart from the administrative cost of running the DPA, another important cost which the workshop discussed at length was the implementation and upkeep of such things as the computer operating system. Until codes of practice have been defined, it would not be clear how quickly one had to respond to a demand for access to a record, or how to respond. Would, for instance, a letter be adequate, and if so, would it be regarded as secure? Access via visual display units would be more secure and could have an effect on costs.

More concern than anything else was expressed on the possible need to adapt existing operating systems which may not have security safeguards and which could be expensive to adapt. Adaptation may also be quite difficult, being clumsy and almost invariably unsatisfactory in performance. It may therefore be necessary to provide dispensations until an installation can start with a clean sheet, using an operating system designed with all the legal requirements in mind. Conversely, it was noted that users were frequently forced to change systems at unnatural times by vendors who market non-compatible systems, and it hardly seemed reasonable to complain about a change at an unnatural time due to data privacy legislation.

It was quite clear, though, that the biggest problem is with timing, and that the eventual cost to users will depend on the lead time between the legislation and the date of implementation. There was some concern that a code of practice might place some responsibility on a user when the problem really lay with the operating system supplied by the vendor.

There was also some concern that multinational companies attempting to run the same system in different countries might have difficulties with varying legislation.

Another problem area which could affect costs was the probable need for an audit trail (i.e. a log of access to the file). The DPC had already noted that an audit trail could eventually be larger than the information file itself. At the same time the audit trail also required protection from interference or corruption. In practice, one needs to have operational copies of files for back-up purposes. It may be necessary to have a control of on the number of copies and to know with certainty where they all are. It may also be necessary to have control of the making of back-up copies to ensure that only the requisite number of copies are made. But how does one ensure that no-one has made a copy of a copy?

There is also a problem with updating of back-up copies, should someone prove his record requires corrections.

Another type of user problem concerns the question of identification of the user seeking access to his record. Clearly, one of the largest groups of users — the local authorities — has the biggest problems to face with privacy legislation because of conflicting requirements. A representative of LAMSAC joined the professional computer organisations in giving an enthusiastic welcome to the report as it stands, stating that it was both reasonable and flexible, although he wondered about the potential gap between a sensible report and an emotive debate in Parliament. However, he was concerned about the mechanics of the problem, particularly the costs outside the data processing department. One aspect of possible legislation concerns the requirement to use information only for the purpose for which is was collected. For instance, although data are collected annually to establish a voting register, it is also very convenient to use the same data to select jurors.

The report proposes a requirement to keep records accurate, which implies regular updating. Yet, in many applications there is no need to update a file frequently in spite of changes which may be held in suspense. Clearly, one can easily lose a level of efficiency if care is not taken with the codes of practice. In local authorities there is a real need to pass information from one department to another, or even one local authority to another. If legislation makes this impossible the loss of efficiency will mean high costs. Additional costs arising from privacy legislation are likely to be increased further where minis are involved.

Another view is that a large part of user costs were likely to be concerned with security of data, which can make an impact at three levels — the physical security of the installation, file integrity and fiscal security. There is a recognised low level of security in many UK installations and it would be useful for DP management to concern itself with operating system integrity for fiscal security alone, apart from what may be necessary for privacy reasons.

Finally, one aspect of cost, although real, may never be evaluated: the time management will have to spend studying the legislation. If the DPC report is widely accepted in industry and commerce, we need to move to legislation as soon as possible. Otherwise, the UK will not be in a bargaining position in discussions in the EEC on harmony of legislation and we might thus lose the benefits of the work done.

2.8 Computers and the Cost of Privacy Laws

Background paper by
Edward Cluff and Professor Paul Samet,
Director, University of London Computer Centre.

The report of the committee on Data Protection shows very clearly that the committee was very sensitive on the question of cost of potential privacy laws. The Summary of the report states that: 'We have concluded that, if implemented in accordance with our recommendations, the scheme of regulation which we propose need not impose unreasonable costs on anyone — users, data subjects or the public purse'.

The report throughout favours a very flexible approach to regulation and clearly the committee believes that such flexibility will avoid undue costs, for example: '.... the unsoundness of any regulatory scheme that includes the universal application of any single requirement by the DPA, e.g. that all subjects of every personal information application should always be notified on their inclusion and sent a copy of their record'. The evidence also shows that, if a sufficiently flexible approach were adopted, it would be possible to devise a system of control by which each of the very different organisations included in our study could meet reasonable data privacy requirements at moderate costs.

Since the majority of commentators in the news media have failed to grasp an essential point in the report, it is possible that others may miss it. This is that the committee has taken note of representations made to it by representatives of professional people in the industry, and that it is the *users* of computers who are going to be involved in the privacy regulations and codes of practice, whilst those employed in the installations will be, quite properly, concerned with the security of the data held on file. It is possibly this more than anything else which may make the prospective legislation manageable and thus control any increase in costs. Furthermore, the committee has reported that 'in our case-studies there often seemed to be more potential for breach of data protection safeguards in the clerical handling and preparation of data preceding automation, and in the security of computer output in its various forms such as printout and microfilm, than in the computer operations themselves. In all these auxilliary processes, the problems of security and access control were greater than within the machine itself, and it seems that problems of regulation are more likely to occur at these weaker points in the system'.

The committee accepted another point submitted to it by representatives of professional people in the industry which can significantly affect costs. This is to establish a hierarchy of security measures to be taken in accordance with the sensitivity of the data. The report accepts that: 'It would be impossible to devise a single set of security requirements with which all users handling personal data could reasonable be required to comply'. It notes that: 'The sensitivity of banking data differs from that of mail order data, and statistical aggregations do not have the same privacy risks as medical histories'. The report accepts that: 'A proper level of security is most important if data protection is to be realised. Whilst privacy is conceptual, security is factual and we believe that the DPA and not the legislation must determine what is required for the different circumstances of users and their applications'.

The report poses some idea of potential costs. Firstly, it rejects licensing in favour of registration on the grounds that 'a licence necessarily condones an element of approval' and that any investigation prior to giving formal approval 'would be excessively expensive in manpower and resources, and would confirm the fears of those who thought that our recommendations would be the occasion for a major extension of bureaucracy'. The scheme of compulsory registration which is recommended in the report will relate to applications and not files as many people feared. Registration will be supplemented by codes of practice with 'different codes .... prepared for different classes of personal data handling applications'.

The report provides 'a guess' of 20,000 such applications by 1980. With an estimated annual cost of the Data Protection Authority of some £520,000, an average charge of £26 per application per annum might be made for universal registration of all 20,000 applications, or £260 per annum with selective registration of, say, only 10% of user applications.

Of course, in many, if not all, cases, the annual registration fee would not be the only cost incurred by the users. One other cost which concerns many people is that of giving the data subject the opportunity to see his record, check it and if necessary have it corrected. The report states that 'the order of cost required to provide the subject with access to his record was found to depend on whether the user was required to supply printouts or copies to every data subject to only to those who asked, whether demand for access was high or low, how much time the user was allowed in order to comply with a request, whether the user has to search only a single file or to extract copies of records about the data subject from several distinct computer files, whether any manual records associated with the computerised file also had to be copied to the data subject, and whether the user was already in regular correspondence with the data subject in the ordinary course of the transactions between them'.

Suggestions made to the committee about the amount to be charged for subject access varied between 50p and £2.50 whilst the report recommends 'that each code of practice should specify the circumstances under which users who are obliged to provide access facilities and a copy of a record, may be allowed to charge a reasonable fee if they wished to do so'.

The intent of the Data Protection Committee is possibly summarised in one key sentence in its report which states, 'Users should be able to handle personal data in the pursuit of their lawful interests or duties to the extent and for the purposes made known or authorised without undue extra cost in money or other resources'.

2.9 Privacy, Defamation and Privilege

Jim Michael, Lecturer in Law,
Polytechnic of Central London

One of the most common objections raised to giving people the right to see records kept on them is that they might sue. Specifically, they might sue for defamation if they didn't like what was written about them in the records. Chapter 32 of the Lindop Report provides a good basic summary of defamation law as it might affect personal records, whether handled by computers or otherwise.

It is important to emphasise that the truth of what is written is a defence to civil actions for defamation (although if the action is a prosecution for criminal libel the only defence is that it was true *and* that the communication was justified in the public interest). But the truth of the statement must be proved, which, as the Lindop Report points out, can be difficult.

The Lindop Committee recommended that 'computer users should be entitled to the defence of qualified privilege if — but only if — such a defence would be available to them if no computer were involved'. Such a privilege is, as the Committee's Report points out, 'reserved for .... situations where the public interest requires that people should be able to speak their minds freely, provided they honestly believe that what they say is true, and do not abuse the occasion for some improper purpose'.

There is one statement in the Lindop report which might be misinterpreted. In explaining qualified privilege, the Report says (para. 32.06): 'All such communications would be severely hampered if every potential D (defendant) had to risk losing an expensive libel action whenever he said or wrote something to X (a third person) which P (a data subject plaintiff) might consider defamatory of himself.' D would only lose the action if what he wrote actually could be proved to be defamatory, that is if a reasonable man would think the worse of P because of it, and if it were false. It perhaps should be pointed out that legal aid is not available for defamation actions, and that if P lost he would normally have to pay his own legal costs and those of D.

If people were entitled to see records kept on them, one likely result would be legal actions to determine more precisely in just what 'situations' the public interest requires such qualified privilege. Many recorded defamatory statements are not now tested to see whether they would be protected by qualified privilege, because the people they are made about never get to see them.

If something is written which is defamatory, and if it is protected by qualified privilege, then the person who wrote it does not need to prove that it was true. The person who wrote the defamatory record is safe so long as he or she honestly believed that it was true, was not 'reckless' about whether it was true or not, and did not write it for an improper 'malicious' purpose.

The key to qualified privilege is not what is in the defamatory record, but the 'occasion' of the communication. In other words, if D (the defendent) writes something defamatory about P (the plaintiff) to X (another person) that may be protected by qualified privilege. But it may lose that qualified privilege if X passes it on to Y, and made X liable to P under the ordinary law of defamation.

Qualified privilege will apply to an occasion if there is a common interest between D and X, and if there is a common duty between them to give their honestly-held opinions. Bankers, employers, and educational establishments are examples of those considered by law to have such common interests and duties in giving each other their honestly-held opinions about debtors, employees, and students, even if those opinions are defamatory and cannot be proved to be true.

It is up to Parliament and the courts to decide just when the public interest justified the protection of qualified privilege. The Lindop Report gives an illustration of how finely the line can be drawn between those occasions which are protected and those which are not. Credit references are subject to qualified privilege if they are between members of a 'mutual' trade protection society, but not if they are from a commercial credit reference agency which sells the information.

Deciding what communications are to be protected by qualified privilege is balancing the public interest in communicating honestly held opinions (even if they are defamatory and false) against the public interest in protecting the reputations of individuals against such false defamatory statements. In the United States the Constitutional protection of freedom of the press has been interpreted as giving greater weight to free comment than to individual reputations on many occasions. In the *New York Times* v. *Sullivan* the Supreme Court held that, in effect, printing false and defamatory allegations against a 'public figure' was protected by qualified privilege. That is not a part of English defamation law, and was rejected by the Faulks Committee in 1975.

But the qualified privilege doctrine in this country has important implications for those who keep records on individuals. Security of personal records could determine whether or not the privilege is kept or lost. For example, if defamatory information in such records is available to those who are merely interested, as opposed to those who have a legally-defined 'interest', then such availability would not be protected. If data subjects had the right to see the records kept on them, and if they could learn who else had seen them, then the courts might be presented with many more cases in which to decide how far qualified privilege should extend.

For example, a communication from one doctor to another about a patient would almost certainly be privileged, but if the information were passed on to a social worker, an employer, or a credit reference agency the public interest in continuing the privilege might be less clear.

The principles recommended by Lindop are useful guidelines for users of personal data who want to avoid losing qualified privilege. Personal data should be accurate and complete, and relevant and timely for the purpose for which they are used;' 'Personal data should be handled only to the extent and for the purposes made known when they are obtained, or subsequently authorised;' 'No more personal data should be handled than are necessary for the purposes made known or authorised.'

Unlike the enforcement sanctions recommended by Lindop, which will depend on legislation and Codes of Practice, the law of defamation is an existing sanction to encourage users to see that personal information is accurate, and, if it is not accurate, that it is circulated only to those who have an interest in receiving it something like a 'need to know'. If 'data subjects' are given enforceable rights to see such records (as they already have been under the Consumer Credit Act 1974) the exact definition of qualified privilege may be determined more exactly in legal actions brought by data subjects themselves.

2.10 The Data Protection Committee Report: Questions and Discussion

Alan Benjamin, Director General, Computer Services Association:

Very briefly, we think the DPC Report is workable, because it depends on the rationality of Codes and, providing there is enough consultation in the framing of those Codes, it is likely to be workable. Secondly, we think it is fair, because it does not penalise users just because they use personal data. It is the use of the data that is attacked, not the file. Thirdly, we think it is potentially inexpensive. That again a little bit is Code-dependent and application-dependent, and it may be that the more sensitive of files and uses will be more expensive. Fourthly, we think it is balanced, because it does not suppress the technology. There is a balance between the data user and the data subject.

One of the things we think that the report underplays is the fact that there are some positive aspects of having a Data Protection Authority to whom one can turn for guidance before you enter the use of personal data. We suspect that the amount of work that the authority might do in this area has probably been underestimated.

Then we think that it has under-emphasised the fact that security is often much firmer and better-structured on a computer than if it is off a computer. That has been, in our view at least, almost ignored.

Finally, we think there are some problems in the compliance checking area. We are not quite sure whether they have thought that one through completely. Whether it spreads through to the auditors in the normal way and whether those auditors are qualified to do so is another matter. That is a nut-shell summary.

CHAIRMAN: Edward G. Cluff, Institute of Data Processing Management:

Before opening up to the audience, I should like to give Joe Jacob an opportunity. I know that he took a leading part in the workshop discussion, but I think we should give you an opportunity to make a few comments on what you think of the DPC Report.

Joe Jacob, Lecurer in Law, LSE;
Member, NCCL Privacy Sub-committee:

I do not think the Report spells out clearly enough the dangers which this conference and the report is about. I thought Charles Read did it much more clearly and if we had that kind of trenchant comment in the report, it would have been a much clearer report, because the mischief would have been much clearer. The problems are to do with the interface of the individual against the large organisation. What the report is trying to do is to balance the interests of the individual against the interests of the large organisation and the interests that the individual has in the proper running of the large organisation. It is a difficult and complex equation to run and, to a large extent, I accept the balance that the DPC has achieved. The reason I do that is that they have come out with a very similar result to what the NCCL was saying eight years ago. And if we were right then I do not see why we should not be prepared to congratulate others on agreeing with us almost a decade later.

My criticism related to the type of controls they had; first, as regards the independence of the DPA from government and the questions of accountability. It seems to me, reading that report, using my knowledge of the way the constitution works and how decisions are made in government and who influences whom and how, that the machinery that they have established gives the Home Secretary all the control that any right-minded, efficient bureaucrat called the Home Secretary would ask for, rather than creating controls against that type of activity.

The third point I raised was the question of civil remedies. Suppose, just for example, the Code on the police file provided that there was to be no linkage between the police file and the Swansea file, and it transpired that there was such a linkage as at the present moment. The report says that the individual can sue for damages. At present, the damages that he would get for that are nominal damages, because he has suffered no pecuniary loss simply because of that linkage. It seemed to me that it makes a nonsense of creating a new civil remedy unless you are going to give it substantive teeth to give the individual an incentive to sue and the incentive for the police — and Swansea — to take some notice of the Code of Practice. Unless you do that, it seems to me that you are creating a toothless tiger.

What I am saying is, in general terms, if there is an abuse of the Code of Practice that does not give rise to direct pecuniary loss, is it right that the individual should have no effective civil remedy to prevent it and to recover substantial damages in that situation? Perhaps the civil law should take into account, say, for example, the injury to feelings arising from undue record linkage. Perhaps it should be dealt with through the criminal law instead.

Professor Paul Samet, Director,
University of London Computer Centre:

I have a few general comments and I have one question for Trudy Hayden as well. One thing that strikes me as a general trend is that, whenever a particular operation becomes easy which was difficult and expensive beforehand, any method that you previously had for controlling it becomes terribly difficult to enforce and to keep enforcing. For instance, copyright was a manageable thing as long as the only way of making copies was by people writing documents — copying it out by hand. Once you have photocopiers, which will produce things very quickly and very cheaply, it is a rather different thing. Once cassette recorders are cheap enough that a large part of the population can buy them, saying that there is a copyright on music and so on is a rather difficult thing to enforce. You might say it, but it is difficult to enforce. I think what we have got at the moment is that a whole lot of information collecting and handling which has been done in the past with a certain amount of difficulty, has actually become a lot easier. I think this is why people are worried, and I think it is a general thing.

A thing that worries me, and I do not see anything in the DPC Report about it, is that a great deal of the public attitude to information handling seems to be based on fear. You always assume that the worst will happen. I know that the worst very often does happen, but there are a lot of occasions when things can be done on behalf of people which could not be done before. I think perhaps a certain amount of education would be a good thing.

There is a certain amount of comment in the report that some very sensitive things, such as religion, race and so on — information about that — should not be kept in some of these files. I think you have got to be very careful to make sure that you do not pass laws which later on you find prevent you from doing things which are actually in the public interest. If you are not allowed to have information about race, religion and so on, you can get the National Front or anybody else making allegations which you know are false but which you have no way of rebutting, because you have not been allowed to collect the information. I think that would be a rather stupid situation to get into.

The question I have for Trudy Hayden is this. She mentioned, among the many problems, enforcement problems. Are the enforcement problems with your privacy laws actually any different from the enforcement problems of other laws which cover difficult and novel situations such as anti-discrimination laws?

Trudy Hayden, former Director, Privacy Project American Civil Liberties Union:

My first answer to you before was probably not, in that we have always had to devise new means of solving problems of individual rights against the state. The more I have had time to think about that, the more I think it might, in the United States, be different. The reason is that the courts have been so hostile to questions of information privacy — so incredibly obtuse about it — particularly the Supreme Court where some unbelievable decisions have come down when they are dealing with information privacy as opposed to the traditional kinds of privacy questions like searches, wire-tapping, and that kind of thing, that the kinds of devices that we have managed to work out for things like anti-discrimination problems just will not do because the courts are not responsive. The kind of licensing authority that they have in Sweden simply would not go down in the United States. It has been discussed a number of times and it has always been rejected with great horror for whatever reasons, and so I am beginning to worry, in fact, that it is a unique problem. I am sure there is a solution somewhere, but I have not the foggiest notion what it is.

Hugh Pitcher, National Computing Centre Ltd:

I should just like to take a point that Joe Jacob mentioned about the civil remedy. He used the words 'pecuniary damage'. What the report says is 'ascertainable damage'. Whether injury to feelings can be regarded as ascertainable in the legal sense, I do not know, but the purpose of this paragraph appears to be to give a court the possibility of recompensing a person for damage other than financial that he suffers.

Joe Jacob:

I am not sure it is. I think ascertainable damage, as I read it, is that, if, for example, there is a breach of a Code related to employment practices and a man loses his job, the damage that flows from that is loss of earnings set off against whatever new job he gets at whatever lesser rate it is than the job he had before, and so forth — ascertainable damage in the common law sense. I am not aware that the words 'ascertainable damage' — certainly not automatically — carry with them the kind of meaning that I would like to attach to that damage.

The kind of thing I have in mind is what the NCCL put forward in 1971. We said that, in making any order which would include the award of damages, the court tribunal 'shall have regard to all the circumstances, in particular to the effect of the collection, storage or use of the information on the health, welfare, social, business or financial position of the individual about whom it is stored or his family'. None of that is really encompassed in the expression 'ascertainable damage', and if you want to extend the common boundaries of what is damage awardable in the court, you have to do it directly by statute. Otherwise, the courts are inevitably and rightly going to apply the criteria that they have been developing since Henry II's day. It seems to me that if we are talking about a new type of damage that Parliament and we are just discovering, we need a new definition of 'damage' as well.

Question:

Can I come back to your original point, because it seems to me that there are two possibilities. Assuming that the DPC Report goes through, that the Code of Practice is set up and the Code of Practice says that files on database A may not be linked to files on database B. If in fact they are so linked, they quite clearly recommend here that if an individual suffers — he presumably suffers pecuniarily in some way or other — if, for example, he loses his job, as you have given in your example, he has a right to sue. If in fact no-one suffers, then surely the proposals in chapter 19, paras. 89—95, show a criminal offence. For example, if you are going to presuppose that a file containing 10 million names is linked to another file, it would be ridiculous to allow all 10 million people to sue, because that is just a redistribution of income.

Joe Jacob:

I am sure Trudy Hayden could tell you about the American class action which would encompass such phenomena. Certainly, the use of administrative measures to control bureaucracy is one thing; the use of criminal back-up, whether it is prosecuted by the police or by the DPA or by anybody else, is another. Citizens do not commonly bring private prosecutions. Commonly they do not bring civil actions either, but the civil action is more common than the criminal one. And it is to the civil courts that I think most citizens would look if they looked to the courts at all for their own initiative. One thing you get in a civil court if you bring the action and win, is the damage and profits for yourself. If you go to prosecute in a criminal court you do not get anything out of it. So that the use and the balance between the civil and criminal law to support the administrative back-up that we are talking about.

Question:

If we are concerned in particular about the public sector, I would suggest that there is more fear in general about public sector files — it is far better, surely, that there should be criminal sanctions against the people in charge of those public sector databases and computer installations than fines which will, in the nature of bureaucracy, only be inflicted against the state. It does not matter. If I run a system and I know that my organisation is going to lose money, well bad luck; but if I may go to prison I am going to be much more careful.

Joe Jacob:

The prospect of sending the chief superintendent in charge of the national police computer to prison for linking with Swansea, whatever the Codes may say, unless it is a flagrant fourth time, seems to be absolutely zero. Far better, it seems to me, to make him answer to his superiors for the damages that they are having to fork out. I do not want to get too involved in the nature of the civil remedy. It was only one criticism amongst a number of others. What I am far more interested to hear from this audience is whether they agree with the report and say, with myself, that there is a danger; whether they agree with me that the report has not spelt out the danger sufficiently; and how they would spell out the kind of problems we are trying to deal with. It seems to me to be far more central to the issues than the precise nature of the legislative or legal controls or abuses after the event.

Question:

I was in fact going to make the same point, that there are criminal sanctions. I do not wish to take it much further in view of what has already been said. But I think it is relevant to say that it envisages that the court will have power to order the user to stop the application, whatever it is. Surely this would be the purpose of any sanctions or any procedures which might be taken to stop the misuse and the power reserved to have that misuse stopped.

Joe Jacob:

I think they have not said enough about the kind of injunctive relief that can apply. Whether, for example, if the Code says you can only give this information to Class A of people and it is given to Class B, you get a remedy for that, whether you can stop that by injunction. Probably you can. Or whether it says you can give it to Class A and they give wrong information; whether you can compel the data user to supply the correct information to the class that he was allowed to supply the information to in the first place. The report is silent on that. That sort of spelling out of the particular types of injunctive relief seems to me to be absolutely essential if the public are going to have any confidence at all in the kind of operation that we are talking about establishing.

Hugh Pitcher:

I Just want to say that the report gives plenty of scope for people to challenge data users in the name of the law. They can ask the DPA to prosecute and the DPA can prosecute if the data user is abusing data. Somebody suggested the possibility of the Chief Constable going to prison. He can only do that in the report if he breaches a court order to improve his ways. A mere breach of a Code of Practice does not lead to imprisonment. It is only if he is ordered by a court to remedy. Can I just read a short passage which may be helpful. It is talking about some people's feelings about privacy: 'That response may strike many as surprising, and even irrational, but people's feelings in such matters are facts which any scheme of regulation concerned with protecting privacy must at least be able to take into account.' That seems to me to show that the DPC has been very conscious that people's feelings are part of the balance which must be struck.

Question:

I should just like to say that perhaps we are over-simplifying the problem to some extent about the linking of files, because databases are one set of data and can be construed as a number of files. Perhaps some of us can remember Mr McNulty's talk in which he showed, rather alarmingly I think, the overall irresponsibility which had dogged some parts of the computer industry. I think the industry really is immature in its relationship with society, and as such, has grown up very quickly and has been unable to keep in step — or rather, society has been unable to keep in step. I think that one positive thing that the report and, hopefully, subsequent Acts, will do will be to impose more overall discipline on the computer community and the use of technology than has been possible by the various associations in the computer industry in the past.

Question:

I want to ask the NCCL, so perhaps Joe Jacob can answer. It is about their concern about police intelligence gathering computers. Can you explain how the data protection regulations will alleviate your concern about those computers?

Joe Jacob:

I am not the NCCL! For a start, nothing at all is said in the specific. It is all down to whatever Code of Practice is eventually devised, so I can give you no concrete answer, except to say that we are in the lap, not of the gods, but at least of the appointees of such. Secondly, if the Code of Practice were to be drafted by the NCCL executive, it would make provision for certain types of information on the police file to be available to the citizen on request. For my part, I would like to see criminal records available to the citizen on request, and I have known cases where criminal records have been wrong and citizens have been subjected to very considerable harassment because wrong evidence has been given in court relating to their previous convictions which has been the basis of the sentence.

Questioner:

I am talking about intelligence gathering — the computerised gossip.

Joe Jacob:

So far as the computerised gossip goes, the NCCL would say that large parts of that have got no part in the state's considerations at all. It is no concern of the state whether I am a member of the Hunt Saboteurs Committee. It is no concern of the state whether I am an executive member of the NCCL. It is no concern of the state whether I am a member of a trade union.

Questioner:

But what effect will the regulations have on that?

Joe Jacob:

The regulations ought to prevent each of those items, by general category, being included. At the present moment the indications are that those who define security risk define it in such a way as to mean that citizens simply do not have a right to control in any effective way the kind of information being gathered and being used — and the chilling effect of the police authorities knowing about one's political or social activities can be very inhibiting in terms of ordinary activity. The 'chilling effect' of lawful activities being disclosed to those to whom it really does not matter at all is really quite frightening.

Tony Bunyan
Director, State Research:

I would say two things. I back up the point about individuals having the right of access to what is held on them, on the intelligence system, but this is the proviso I want to bring in now — providing that it exists. We are dealing with a situation here, whether you are talking about actual intelligence held on the national police computer or this particular computer — the Metropolitan National Intelligence Computer — or the Thames Valley Project or the records held by the security services. We are talking about a situation which is so far down the road and has been going on for so many years, which has been set up without any consultation with Parliament — Parliament has been informed, very often via the press about what is happening. And you enter a very critical area. On the one hand, you have to start to say that the operations of the police have to come under Parliamentary control, which would be to reverse something like 100 years of our British history. And secondly, you have got to say that the kind of information which the security services are allowed to gather on political and industrial activity has got to be limited to those who are a real danger to all the people, and not extended to those who hold particular views or who undertake particular actions which are not popular to those who run the state at the moment. So I am actually saying that it is a much wider question than what kind of safeguards you have on your computers. It is even much wider than citizens having access. It has to go back to the kind of brief which these agencies and which the police have had. They have used this freedom — this lack of democratic discussion and control — and it is much wider than a single question about how a Code of Practice can define it. A Code of Practice cannot define it. The problem lies elsewhere, and we are only dealing with the end product, not with the real cause.

Question:

I think one has to keep in mind section 8.02 of the report which says 'keep it in perspective'. I am afraid that on this we seem to have developed way outside data protection in suggesting that somewhere there is a law which says that you shall do nothing without either going back to Parliament or getting public approval. And one would ask many people in business and many people in other occupations or organisations how they would exist if such was the case. I would like to correct that impression. The feeling one is left with is that there was a requirement for consultation going back to make any change on the police side. All I am reminding anyone, of course, is the way the committee came down in 8.02.

Joe Jacob:

I do not think it is a matter of saying that you cannot do things that are not specifically authorised. When you say 'keep it in perspective' that is precisely what the NCCL has been trying to do since 1934. It has been trying to determine what the perspective is, and it is the secrecy about not knowing what files are held that makes us very suspicious as to what the perspective is that we are being asked to keep it in.

Section 3
Employment Records
3.1   Personnel Records and References

Society of Civil and Public Servants

Employment records, as they are compiled today, involve an accumulation of information on employees which can cover not only an appraisal of work performance but also criminal, political and sexual activities. The practices surrounding the recording of these details, however, vary considerably according to the type and sphere of employment. In most areas of private employment there is little information available on these practices. Consequently, this paper concentrates mainly on the situation in the Civil Service.

Work Assessment

In the Civil Service work assessment is carried out by an immediate superior and is in the form of an annual *Confidential* Report. These reports contain an assessment of an individual's performance and a statement as to whether he/she is suitable for promotion.

Since 1971 the Civil Service unions have been negotiating for the replacement of this system by one whereby the employee concerned would have the opportunity to see and comment on his/her report. In March 1978, a new agreement was finally reached which, although not providing for open reporting in any complete form, goes some way in improving the situation.

Basically, it provides a comprehensive national framework for the disclosure of annual report *markings* by entitling those who so request, to receive their overall performance and their assessment of promotability marking. There is a provision for all aspects of the report (apart from the section dealing with long term potential) to be communicated orally to the individual and there is an entitlement for the individual to have recorded any disagreement she/he wishes to register regarding this information Lastly, the agreement requires that the information communicated must be in the context of a structured interview. The unions, although accepting the new agreement, are continuing to press for full open reporting.

Criminal Records

Apart from these assessment records, information on employees is also obtained through police records. Criminal records are routinely forwarded to employers in government agencies and to certifying professional bodies. Instructions from the Home Office Police Department require local police forces to communicate the details of convictions. Table 3 from *Private Lives and Public Surveillance*, by James B. Rule shows the details of these practices in a number of government agencies.

This list is far from complete and does not take into consideration the police records on people who have never been convicted of an offence. *Private Lives* points out how far-reaching Britain's system of recording is and how relatively accessible individuals' records are to employers who are looking for information on either current or prospective employees.

Table 3. Reporting of Convictions by Police to Outside Agencies.

Persons on whom convictions are reported	Nature of convictions reported	To whom reported
Civil Servants and employees of Atomic Energy Authority	all convictions, except minor traffic offences	Civil Service Dept. for transmission to employing department
Justice of the Peace	all convictions	Lord Chancellor's office
Solicitors or solicitors' clerks	any offence involving money or property	The Law Society
Teachers	offences of a nature which may render them unsuitable for teaching or care of children	Home office
Registered Medical Practitioners	All offences for which the *maximum* penalty is imprisonment for one month without the option of a fine or greater	General Medical Council
State Certified Midwives		General Midwives Board
Registered Dental Practitioners		Dental Board of the United Kingdon
State Registered Nurses, Enrolled Assistant Nurses, Student Nurses, and Pupil Assistant Nurses		General Nursing Council

Source: Home Office Circular No. 151/1954; No. 77/1955; No. 11/1961 and No. 4/1969

Political Activities

In addition to access to police records, the Civil Service has a security system whereby certain employees are checked for 'subversive' connections. Positive Vetting, as it is called, was first introduced in 1952. It involves (a) checking with Security Service records for 'adverse information'; (b) the completion of a detailed security questionnaire; (c) a thorough field investigation, which attempts (through interviews with past teachers and former employers, etc.) to build up a complete picture of a subject's life back to his/her school days. In 1954 this procedure was broadened and strengthened to apply to a wider grouping of people — all those who came into contact with 'sensitive areas' — and to include checking not only for membership of or association with 'subversive' organisations, but also for 'serious character weaknesses of a kind which might make a person subject to blackmail'. In addition, a much lower standard of proof was required. This procedure is essentially the same one that is operating at present in the Civil Service. Security requirements, along with detailed questions concerning health, family, etc, accompany most application forms for the Civil Service. The following sentence comes from a General Information Booklet which is given to applicants for Executive Officer posts: 'Nobody may be employed in security work who is or has recently been a member of the British Communist Party or of a Fascist organisation'.

Employment Records in Other Areas

Work Assessment

According to a recent survey involving 288 organisations from private and public industries, which was conducted by the Institute of Personnel Management, nearly two-thirds of the companies surveyed did not disclose assessment reports in full to the individuals concerned. Only 39% of the companies practised open reporting; 35% disclosed reports in part, but the section on future potential promotion prospects was usually not disclosed; and 26% of the companies did not disclose the reports at all.

Blacklists

As in the public sector, private sector employers accumulate detailed information on their current and prospective employees. The compiling of blacklists, i.e. a list of people who for various reasons are not considered to be suitable for employment, has become a common means of determining whether or not to employ an individual. The two best known examples are the Department of Education and Science's blacklist of teachers and youth workers, and the Economic League's blacklist of trades unionists.

The DES, together with the Scottish and Welsh Offices, in accordance with regulations made under the Education Act 1944, maintains 'List 99', a blacklist of people who may not be employed as teachers or in the youth service. In 1976 the list contained about 1,200 names of people either completely banned from teaching or able to teach only in specific fields of education. A teacher can be banned following a criminal conviction; for misconduct which can include sexual approaches to a pupil or another child or to an adult of the same sex; for conduct 'inappropriate to a teacher' or excessive use of the cane. The Economic League, a private organisation funded by industry, maintains a central register of political and trade union activists which more than 4,500 firms use to vet prospective employees. The Economic League, which was founded in 1919, provides information to subscriber firms on alleged 'subversives' in trades unions in order to exclude militants from employment.

Legal Rights

Access to Employers' Records

In recent cases of *Nasse versus the Science Research Council* and *Vyas versus Leyland Cars Ltd*, the issue of the right of access to information held on employees has been taken up legally. The cases involved alleged discrimination on the grounds of race, sex and trade union activity. Both complainants sought the disclosure of employment records under the powers given to courts and tribunals to order disclosure of documents needed for an applicant's case. Mrs Nasse applied to an industrial tribunal on two grounds: '(a) discrimination against me for carrying out trade union activity; and (b) discrimination against me because I am a married woman'. She requested the discovery of the annual confidential report of two of her colleagues. The Industrial Tribunal granted an order that the Council make available such documents and the Employment Appeal Tribunal dismissed the Council's appeal against this order.

Mr Vyas alleged that Leyland had discriminated against him because of his race. As in the Nasse case, he applied to the Industrial Tribunal for orders for further particulars and discovery, requesting a wide range of information. The Industrial Tribunal ordered Leyland to provide information concerning the employment records of three other employees, but declined to order Leyland to produce information which they had received in confidence. Mr Vyas appealed to the Employment Appeal Tribunal, which allowed the appeal and ordered the discovery. Both the Council and Leyland appealed to the Court of Appeal, which overruled the decisions of the EAT. The Court of Appeal ruled: 'The Industrial Tribunals should not order or permit the disclosure of reports or references that have been given and received in confidence except in very rare cases where, after inspection of a particular document, the Chairman decides that it is essential in the interests of justice that the confidence should be overriden; and then only subject to such conditions as to the divulging of it as he shall think fit to impose, both for the protection of the maker of the document and the subject of it.' The Court of Appeal decision has severely limited the right of access to employment records.

In the Nasse case, however, the Council voluntarily furnished Mrs Nasse with her own annual confidential reports. Following the Court of Appeal decision, the Civil Service unions have suggested to the Civil Service department that there should be a regular procedure in Industrial Tribunal cases involving discrimination on grounds of sex, race or trade union activity to disclose the annual reports. The CSD has replied that if an individual alleging discrimination sought disclosure of his or her own report, the department concerned would be prepared to release it.

Blacklists

Although it is unlawful under the Employment Protection Act 1975 for an employer to dismiss an employee for trade union activity, there is no protection for those who are refused a job as a result of being blacklisted. In April 1977, the Employment Appeal Tribunal heard the case of a trade unionist who, knowing that no large organisation would employ him because of his record of trade union activity, gave a false name and reference to Birmingham Corporation. He was recognised and dismissed, but in the following year he was employed at a different site of the same organisation and was again sacked on the ground that, the previous year, he had deceived the employer. The Industrial Tribunal upheld his complaint against unfair dismissal, stating that he was protected against victimisation for taking part in trade union activity. Birmingham Corporation appealed to the Employment Appeal Tribunal, which overruled the decision on the ground that, not having been employed for six months, he was not covered by the law. EAT endorsed the use of blacklists by stating that 'he was dismissed because he was discovered in a dishonest subterfuge to which he resorted in order to get round a *justifiable embargo* against his employment resulting from his activities'.

3.2   Personnel Information Systems in British Airways

Michael Bruce,
Manpower Adviser, British Airways.

British Airways holds a considerable amount of information both about those who fly on its services and those who work for it. Much of this data is of a factual nature and is provided by those whom it describes. The confidentiality of such information is jealously guarded and so far few problems have been experienced in holding it. As British Airways tends to take a corporate stance only on issues that are perceived generally as 'problems' about which there is a need for a unified point of view, the Company has not so far thought it necessary to promulgate any statement of its views on the matter. Commonsense, reasonableness, and a care for the interests of employees are expected from managers in this as in other aspects of their work. British Airways does, however, in common with many other organisations, generate a significant amount of 'soft' opinionative and evaluative information about those who work for it. It is this information that possibly contains the seeds of potential conflict as the Company faces the opposing pressures of respect for the individual, an 'open' style of management, worker participation, and the need to pursue more active manpower policies. This paper describes current practices regarding the information British Airways holds about people and indicates some of the main problems the Company could face in the fairly near future.

Passenger Information

British Airways operates a very large scale passenger reservations system, with 3,500 computer terminals in 23 countries worldwide, handling personal travel data.

This system holds on average 1.2 million records of current passenger itineraries, including additional details such as contact reference, and any special needs (e.g. vegetarian meal), referenced by date of travel, journey and passenger name. These records are accessible to all British Airways reservations staff worldwide, and through them to telephone enquirers having an apparent need or right to the information. Additional confidentiality is accorded to passengers requesting this, by means of a special instruction to this effect within the passenger data record.

The design and operation of the system is based on the premise of improved service resulting from convenient access to information, rather than affording secrecy of individuals' movements, which in the majority of cases are of little concern to others. The experience of 10 years' operation appears to confirm that this is a reasonable approach. British Airways considers that the transfer of its computer files to another organisation for their own use would be improper, and in any event the information is so structured that it would be difficult and expensive to extract much significant information by reprocessing these files. It should, however, be noted that itineraries involving other airlines are automatically transmitted to these airlines, frequently on a computer-to-computer basis.

Without this facility, the present high level of travel service afforded to airline passengers would be enormously diminished. To date, airline passengers woud seem more concerned with the level of service they receive rather than an invasion of their privacy.

Access to the computer system terminals is restricted to authorised personnel, by means of a password 'sign-in' procedure, and all transactions on any selected terminals can be logged (if for example unauthorised use were suspected). The overall number of transactions averages about 1 million daily.

Personal Information held on Staff

A wide variety of information is held within British Airways on its 50,000 UK employees.

a)   There is an integrated Pay, Pensions and Personnel computerised information system covering all staff. Much of the information is of a factual nature and the reports generated by the system are mainly statistical. (See summary on page 68). This information is available to staff, though much of it is held in a form that makes access difficult.

b)   For flying staff there is a computerised on-line information system that holds data which allows staff to be rostered on a very complex set of aircraft schedules, and which keeps track of their overseas movements.

c)   British Airways Medical Service holds extensive medical data on staff, particularly as regards the fitness of flying crew. The medical service follows general medical practice regarding confidentiality of such records and the interpretation of the information to line management.

d)   There is a personnel file on each member of staff. As these files have tended to be used as a method of recording any and every transaction the employee has with the Company, they presently have limited utility as sources of information. The Company is currently examining its personnel administration with a view to standardising and improving practices on a Company-wide basis. Although these files are not generally shown to staff, the general feeling within the Company is that each person should be able to inspect and correct his file.

e)   Both the Personnel and line managers hold a variety of data relating to selection, training, current job performance, professional competence and future employment potential. The way in which such information is held and the extent to which it is open to employee inspection varies from Department to Department. The pattern of communication tends to be very much a reflection of the managerial style of the boss and the relationships he has with his staff. As one manager remarked, 'if relationships are good and the style is open, there really is very little that cannot be communicated to staff'.

Attitudes towards the handling and disclosure of employee information tend to depend on the nature and content of the information under consideration. Few people in the Company would dissent from the view that where basic factual information relating to a staff member's terms and conditions of employment is concerned, the basic principles outlined in Data Protection Committee Report should form the guidelines for its conduct. British Airways certainly would accept full responsibility for the security of the employee data it holds and currently takes great care to prevent unauthorised disclosure. It would also agree that only necessary and relevant information should be recorded and that all information should be regularly reviewed and updated. The tendency has been to define 'relevant' in terms of job relatedness and to avoid any suspicion of prying into the employee's personal life. The Company would also tend to accept that when it wanted to change or add to its personal information requirement that it should consult its employees through the recognised channels.

Few line or personnel managers within the Company would however consider a policy of complete and total disclosure of all information held on an employee to that employee, well advised. Whilst there is a general tendency for managers to move towards an open and participative style of management thus making disclosure more rather than less likely, this change is mediated by the pragmatic concern about the impact that the disclosure of information would have on the person to whom it was revealed. This is particularly the case when it comes to telling the employee how his potential for future employment in the Company is perceived. Whereas most managers, as part of the regular appraisal systems will discuss an employee's current job performance with him and allow the employee to comment in writing on that assessment, future potential would not be revealed even though career guidance is offered when requested. A similarly pragmatic approach can be observed in the Personnel Department's approach to the communication of information to an employee's supervisor. The extent of the communication depends on the nature of the personal qualities of the supervisor. Such an approach and the interpretive role is also followed in the revelation of data gathered through selection tests.

Immediate reaction to the Report of the Data Protection Committee would suggest there is nothing that British Airways as a Company could not comfortably live with, always provided that the Data Protection

Authority conducts its affairs with commonsense and keeps regulation to the minimum necessary for effective action. British Airways would doubtless have to hold data in a way which is accessible and meaningful to staff but this would be no bad thing. It would also have to specify more precisely who had access to information, always a tricky point. No doubt, too, the Company would need to take a clearer and firmer line with those who have a tendency to hoard information long after it has ceased to have any value or indeed meaning. These on the whole are relatively minor problems.

Feeling within British Airways suggest that the more difficult issue is not that of confidentiality but one of privacy. The Company has a highly educated workforce that increasingly demands both a meaningful work environment and that the Company follows active manpower policies regarding the deployment and utilisation of staff to achieve this. Similarly, the active pursuit of positive policies of equality of opportunity move the Company in the same direction. Implementation of such requests is only possible if the Company increases the amount of information it holds on individual staff members. Inevitably there is a reduction in privacy. Perhaps the best that employers can do as they work their ways through the detailed problems posed by these conflicting cross currents, is to ensure that staff are aware of Company practice and ideally fully consent to it.

British Airways — Computerised Personnel Data

British Airways holds personnel data of all its UK ground staff on an integrated Pay, Pensions and Personnel computer system. The system is a batch processing system and is used for all aspects of administration as well as for information purposes.

Staff Number
Surname
First Christian Name
Other Initials
Title (Mr. Mrs. Miss)
Sex/Marital Status
Date of Birth
Date of Engagement
Registered Disabled Indicator
Staff Type, eg UK, Overseas Contract/Area
Contact Address and Telephone Number
Next of Kin (NOK) Relationship
NOK Title
NOK Address

NOK Telephone Number
Date of Marriage
Christian Name, Initials and Date of Birth (Wife)
Sex and Date of Birth of Children (Under 27)
Employment Status (Permanent, Temporary)
Work Location
Industrial Negotiations Group/Agreement (NSP)
Pay Grade
Other Regular Fixed Payments
Date of last Annual Increment
Retirement Date
Organisation Budget Code/Section Code
Increment List Code (internal Pay use)
Job Title
Air Transport and Travel Industry Training Board Code —
  ie Occupational Classification — Knowledge/Skill content
  (eg Systems Analysis) and level of Accountability
  (eg Manager).
Last Overseas Posting Date
Broken/Continuous Service
Date of Appointment to Current Post
Date of Upgrading (ie a change in grade but *no* change in job)
Qualifications — School Academic
                 Higher Academic
                 Apprenticeship/Traineeship
                 Professional
                 City & Guilds
                 Commercial, Technical, Vocational
Engineering Approvals
            Licences
            Training Courses
Language Proficiency
Termination (Date & Reason)
Absence (Dates & Reason)

Some Standard Personnel Information Computer Outputs

1 Staff Strength Manpower Equivalent
  — Distribution of staff numbers by branch, NSP, Contract of
    Employment

2 Overtime Manpower Equivalent
  — Distribution of overtime hours and manpower equivalent by
    Branch, NSP and contract

3 Gummed labels — Home Address
                — British Airways Address

4 Engagements listing
         — Union Membership Agreement Check

5 Transfers Listing

6 General Purpose ad hoc listing — UK staff

7 General Purpose ad hoc listing — Overseas staff

8 Registered Disabled Persons

9 Regular fixed pay elements listing — Foreign language

10 Air Transport & Travel Industry Training Board
    — Occupational Group Summary

11 Absence Analysis — Average Days Lost per employee
    Uncertificated (Under 4 days duration) or Certificated (4 days
    or more)
    — NSP/Sex

12 Absence Analysis — Average Days Lost per employee
    Certificated — over 3 days duration.
    — NSP/Sex

13 Absence Analysis — Pay Grade

14 Absence Analysis — Start Day in relation to Rest Day

3.3 Science and Privacy

Dr. Joseph Hanlon

Scientific careers are sometimes made or broken through totally secret reports. The process is known as refereeing, and is the method by which scientists comment on the work of their peers. It is used both in giving research grants and in deciding if scientific papers should be published. Science is portrayed to the general public as an open and enlightened pursuit of knowledge. In fact, it is sometimes corrupt and usually highly competitive.

Referees are asked by funding agencies and journals to comment on the scientific merit of the work in question - its originality, its accuracy, its completeness, and so on. As with job references, it is usually said that people will be honest and open only if they are assured of anonymity. But since the referees may be competing with the scientists whose work they are commenting on, there is a substantial chance for abuse. Most important, the editors and funding boards rarely know the details of obscure areas of science, so they put considerable trust in referees' reports. Thus, an erroneous or malicious report can seriously damage a scientific career, without the scientist ever knownig what was wrong.

This problem has been debated for some years in the scientific press. Proponents of open refereeing argue that not only would it be more honest and accurate, but that referee's comments might actually help the scientists in question.

The practice varies widely, even within Britain's Research Councils. The Social Science Research Council takes the hardest line — referees are told "Your comments should not be divulged to any other individual or organisation, including the applicant." If a referee were found to have sent a copy of his report to his subject, he would probably be barred from refereeing for SSRC again. The Medical Research Council is less strict than SSRC, but it discourages referees from sending reports to grant applicants. The Science Research Council heads the forms it sends to referees "in confidence" but leaves this to referees to interpret. If asked, it stresses that it is OK for the referee to send a copy of the report to the applicant if he or she chooses. None of the research councils, however, allow applicants to actually see the referee's reports.

In the US, with its Freedom of Information Act, the National Science Foundation has adopted a policy of open refereeing while guaranteeing the privacy of those referees who wish it. Grant applicants may see the reports, but not the names of referees who wrote them.

Scientific journals vary considerably as well. Most discourage contact between referees and authors. But New Scientist, which normally (but not always) sends referee's reports directly to authors, advocated in a leader that referees who believe in open refereeing should adopt it unilaterally, simply by sending copies of reports to subjects no matter what editors and research councils say.

3.4   Report from the Workshop on Employment Records

David Dent, SCICON

The two leaders of the discussion were Mr Michael Bruce, Manpower Adviser of British Airways, who gave a summary of the combined personnel, pay and pensions system employed within British Airways (UK) for their 55,000 employees, and Mr Barrie Sherman, Director of Research at ASTMS, who raised some particular concerns felt both within his own union and other union organisations. These are covered as we go through the various points.

The majority of the other workshop participants were involved directly in employee work in personnel departments, with one or two exceptions, particularly myself. My interest there was both as an observer and also as a potential data subject. I felt that at least the little man ought to have something to say.

It was generally accepted that the information held on a computer personnel system is almost identical within any organisation. There are certain basic details which are kept and, looking at any system, you will find that mostly they are the same.

The discussion covered the question of performance assessments, which, although of a subjective nature, if based on current activities and current performances, could be regarded as part of the basic record. This should possibly be added to the record, with the proviso that it is also included in any information that is passed on to the subject for his own checking. However, it was pointed out that it is common practice for the contents of this record to be circulated to the individual with the option to correct it or comment on it, but this option is very rarely taken up. Whether this means that the records are accurate or that people are not concerned, nobody is quite sure. The only point they ever seem to pick up is if they are being paid too little.

The use of the computer record was discussed, and again, the primary uses, which are mainly statistical, are very similar within different organisations. The only divergence between the uses are in the areas of manpower planning, which clearly involves the use of information other than factual information. There is obviously other information that must be kept, and is kept, about individuals. Some of it is purely back-up written information — letters of offer, letters of acceptance, the original application forms, and some statutory information such as agreement to deductions from salary, which must be retained. Amongst that also will be a certain amount of subjective assessment. This again was a point of some discussion. It was felt that this information is by its very nature, for the use of management and would not normally be disclosed to the employees, since it is obviously a changing piece of information and not necessarily damning. However, it was pointed out that, among the organisations represented, Shell UK certainly made a practice of giving this information, though with the proviso that the employee bear in mind that it was not a once-and-for-all damning marking.

In this area Barrie Sherman was particularly concerned that the application forms which we have all had experience filling in were unnecessarily complicated and contained information which was no use whatsoever for the job involved. It was also a concern that information on application forms, even when the individual was not offered a post with the organisation, became available to third parties. But the organisations represented did not have any cases that they could recall of this happening.

References were not regarded as a major problem. It was felt that, ethically, organisations would only request references when the person concerned knew of the fact. There was concern that, if the content of the reference was pared down to the state that is currently quite common in America of saying 'Yes, Mr Smith did work for us, period', back-up information would be passed by telephone. That would not be acceptable because clearly abuse could be found in this area.

ASTMS is concerned that proliferation of the cheaper computers would mean that information would become more widely available and consequently would become more open to abuse. Discussion here pointed out that the decreasing cost of technology should free more resources to enable the increased level of security at the software level. My own company being involved in the sale of software, it is clear that advances in this are not quite as rapid as the declining cost of technology, but are improving rapidly. With the introduction of codes of practice it is clear that certain additional facilities will be made available.

Generally speaking the report of the DPC found favour with people involved in personnel work and it was felt from what one might call the management side that there would be no great difficulty in arriving at a code of practice. The idea of declaring the use of your data was obviously seen as sound, though any attempt to legislate on what areas may be allowed within the broad subject was not considered to be a good idea.

There was a considerable discussion on the flexibility of the usage that should be defined. Clearly there are management purposes to which the information will be put, and they cannot be specified, chapter and verse, at each occasion they are done. Having to return to the employees or the negotiating committees on every occasion would be impractical, time-consuming, and, of course, would increase the costs.

There were additional concerns expressed by Barrie Sherman, in particular the involvement of third parties, such as credit agencies and similar reference bodies. This was an area of some difficulty. It was felt that the information they supplied was important, although accuracy was difficult to obtain. With the changes in the Consumer Credit Acts of recent years, it was felt that changes in this information would be easier to obtain for the subject concerned.

The general feeling was that the report appeared to cover the area very satisfactorily and would find favour within the personnel department of most major organisations.

Section 4
SOCIAL WORK AND MEDICAL RECORDS

4.1   Social Workers and Their Records
Ron Lacey, Social Work Adviser, MIND (National Association for Mental Health)

Social work has during the past 30 years become a major growth industry. This growth is not only reflected in increased public spending on social services, but also in the increased statutory powers which social workers can now exercise over the citizen. Most of these powers are exercised outside judicial process and any direct form of public scrutiny. In the courts the social worker is now regarded as an expert witness whose records are privileged documents. Their decisions and opinions intrude into areas where the most basic of human rights are at issue. Social workers can remove a child from its parents on the basis of opinion without having to test that opinion by due process. They can remove a patient's right and power in respect of her children, again outside any form of due process. A child in the statutory care of a local authority has no formal means to challenge the validity of the decisions of the "experts" who care for him. He can be diagnosed disturbed, maladjusted or deprived and be placed in a community school, a subnormality ward, a remand centre, a psychiatric ward or an adolescent unit, or whatever. He can be confined in solitary confinement, controlled by drugs or sent to an experimental youth treatment centre — all on the basis of decisions which are made in confidential case conferences. Social workers' decisions to exercise their power, or indeed not to exercise their duties, can determine whether a citizen, be he a child, a psychiatric patient or an elderley person, can be detained by the State against his will. Social workers are literally given a cradle to the grave mandate by a community which has not really asked what social work actually is or how it is done.

Social work represents society's increasing investment in the quality of life. Therefore it is inevitable that it reflects the different and often conflicting value systems in which it operates. At a moral level the community is divided on the issue of whether the deviant is either a sinner or sinned against, mad or bad, etc. etc. At a political level the social services may be seen as a strategy for creating a more egalitarian society, or a means of offering protection and succour to those who are less able to compete in free enterprise market economy. Equally, for some there is too much welfare and for others too little. Thus a confused profession exists in a community which is itself confused as to its expectations of social workers.

The modern social worker is very much the product of his own history. He combines in the present day the roles of the workhouse guardian, the poor law relieving officer, the priest and the psychotherapist or counsellor. He has to reconcile the role of policeman with that of confidante. In one context the information a client gives him is confidential and bound by profesional ethics, in another that same information is the property of the social services to pass on to other officials as they think fit. Consider the implications of the multi-disciplinary clinical team in a psychiatric hospital. Traditionally the patient would assume that any discussions of his condition would be undertaken exclusively within the context of his treatment, and would be bound to confidence by medical ethics. However, the multi-disciplinary team usually includes a local authority social worker who will inevitably on occasions feel that his duties, say to protect a child, would over-ride any rules of confidence applying to the clinical team as a whole. Psychiatric diagnosis may often be a speculative process involving a number of meetings of the multi-disciplinary team. Thus diagnostic speculations as to a person's psychological or emotional state may be given as evidence in a court hearing through the social worker's report. What may be at stake in that hearing is the care and custody of the patient's children. Concern has already been expressed by consultant psychiatrists to MIND about the ambiguities concerning the accountabilities and responsibilities of the members of multi-disciplinary teams.

Given the wide scope of the social work task combined with the confusion as to its methods, it is inevitable that the social worker casts his information net widely. Social workers 'liaise' on a routine basis with the police, the courts, various personnel in the health service such as doctors and health visitors, housing departments, the supplementary benefits officers and occasionally even with the employer of a client. Each of these different agencies pass information to, and receive information from, social services departments. Amongst this information a great deal of opinion will be included, and in the process is likely to achieve the status of fact in a number of procedures to define the eligibility of an individual to benefits and services of different kinds. Thus a social worker may be invited by a housing department to give an opinion on the question as to whether a family should be rehoused or evicted. He may also discuss the question of an extraordinary needs payment with the supplementary benefits office. If a child is suspected by the police of committing an offence, the police juvenile bureau will request information from the social services department as to what is known about that child's home background. A Mental Health Review Tribunal may request a home circumstances report from the social services in order to decide whether or not to discharge a compulsorily detained patient in a mental hospital. There are numerous administrative inter-departmental and inter-agency networks which involve the social services department, through which information passes freely and is translated into decisions affecting the rights of the individual. In day to day practice, however, one significant group is denied access to this information as a matter of policy, namely the individuals about whom the information is held. In an experiment, 10 researchers posing as social workers sought confidential information from 16 agencies: of those only one refused to divulge information over the telephone. (Community Care 23rd May, 1975)

I have already briefly alluded to problems imposed in evaluating and deciding the relevance of information which originates from social workers. The language, jargon, of social work is far from precise in its meaning. Like Humpty Dumpty, when a social worker uses a word 'it means precisely what (he) chooses it to mean - neither more nor less.' Social work has borrowed its language from many sources, psychoanalysis, psychology, sociology psychiatry and Law being the major ones. Thus an individual may be deprived, disturbed, neurotic, paranoid, manipulative, 'at risk', etc. etc. From whatever sources the words are culled, such words undergo an amplification of any pejorative connotations as soon as they enter the language of social work. Thus a client may be described as a paranoid if he suspect the man from the welfare. Another may be described as lacking 'insight' if her views on child rearing differ from those of her social worker. In one court case a child was 'at risk' of being run over by a bus! In another the information that a mother 'reached easy orgasm through mutual masturbation with her homosexual partner' was somehow deemed relevant by a social worker to her capacities to care for her child. These are ludicrous factual examples but they represent the tip of an enormous iceberg of confusion which reigns in social work today. Whilst it is gratifying to note that the Data Protection Committee acknowledges the dubious nature of social work information and urges caution in its interpretation, it is important to acknowledge *now* that there are serious grounds for concern not only about the dissemination of social services information but also about the very nature of that information and its use.

The Younger Committee in their report (Cmnd 5012) laid down ten principles for handling personal information. Compare some of these principles with current practice in social services departments.

Principle 1   Information should be regarded as held for a specific purpose and not be used, without appropriate authorisation, for other purposes.

Principle 2   Access to information should be confined to those authorised to have it for the purpose for which it was supplied.

In practice when a person seeks help from a social services department a single case file is opened and is likely to remain open and available, more or less in perpetuity to any other employee of that department. Thus a couple seeking help with a marital problem from a social services department are likely to do so on the implicit assumption that they are entering into a confidential professional relationship with an individual social worker. This is not so; as soon as a case file is opened it becomes the property of the department. The information on that file may be used in a court of law, may be passed to another department of the authority and so on.

Principle 3   The amount of information collected and held should be the minimum necessary for the achievement of a specified purpose.

Take for example case files in respect to the chronically sick and disabled. It is not uncommon for these files to contain more information on the 'character' of an isolated elderley person, than factual information concerning his practical needs, i.e. housing, medication, heating, extent of physical mobility, actual degree of isolation, etc.

Principle 5   There should be arrangements whereby the subject could be told about any information held concerning him.

Local authorities compile registers of children thought to be at risk by neglect or ill treatment. A person can get put on this register on the basis of anonymous complaints from neighbours or unsupported reports from other sources. It is not the practice that those whose names are included on the 'at risk' registers are informed that this has been done.

The British Association of Social Workers seem to take a very partial approach to the principle that the client should have access to information held concerning him. Their position on this is stated thus:

> Sometimes in the worker's judgement it may be helpful for the client to see his own file, but the file is the property of the agency. In certain circumstances it is a privileged document and a refusal to allow a client, for example the parent of a child in care, access to it would be upheld in a court of law. (BASW. Confidentiality in Social Work.)

In practice the clients of social services departments are seldom, if ever, given access to the files held by social workers concerning them.

Principle 9   Data held should be accurate. There should be machinery for the correction of inaccuracy and the updating of information.

Principle 10 Care should be taken in coding value judgement.

It is precisely in these areas that social work has its greatest difficulties. Is the social worker an expert? Are his definitions of a client's problems to be treated as facts or value judgements by information systems?

The British Association of Social Workers take the view that ultimately it is for the social worker to decide whether or not it is in the client's best interests that he should know the content of the records concerning him held by the agency.

Given that eligibility for certain services or that the liberty of an individual may be decided by the information held by a social services department, this position is clearly unacceptable. MIND takes the view that there may be exceptional grounds for declining to reveal to a client information held concerning him, i.e. sensitive information about a foster parent of a child in care, or information about another member of the client's family may be reasonably withheld to protect the privacy of a person other than the client. However we believe that the social services should have to justify non-disclosure on the basis of commonly agreed principles. We believe it to be entirely unacceptable that the question of what should be disclosed to a client should depend on the social worker's opinion as to what constitutes that client's best interests. The case for this is made even more compelling by the fact that despite their extensive statutory powers social workers are not directly accountable to any public authority other than their employer.

4.2 State of Medical Records
Dr John Dawson, Assistant Secretary
British Medical Association and formerly
Secretary BMA Central Ethical Committee.

Almost ten years ago in 1969 the Association's Board of Science and Education produced a report on the (then) current use of computers in medicine.

The BMA report, a Conservative Research Department paper, and the report of the Younger Committee all stressed the necessity of good security and confidentiality for information committed to automatic data processing systems. In particular, a principle emerged that has been of great recurrent importance — information should only be released and used for the specific purpose for which it was gathered.

The Hospital Activities Analysis run by each NHS region was established in 1970 and the Mental Health Enquiry and the Oxford Records Linkage Study were also operative at this time.

In 1975 a steering committee on Child Health was announced by DHSS and a circular HN (76)6 was issued in January 1976 entitled 'Computer Based Child Health Services, Pre-School System. The circular outlined a proposed provisional version of the standard pre-school system.

The Child Health Computing Committee (CHCC) was convened in April 1976 and included, as had the earlier steering committee, representatives of the BMA.

The purpose of the CHCC was to comment on the description already published and to brief the Welsh Health Technical Services Organisation to develop a batch processing system to record and analyse details of a child's health and to remind parents and health workers when routine surveillance and developmental monitoring exercises should be carried out.

In addition the CHCC intended that information should be available for research and planning purposes. There was no real definition of whether the research or planning had to be germane to the needs of the population from which the original information had been gathered. Local Social Services departments with their diverse responsiblities to other organisations will also be involved. In particular, it was proposed to transfer the notification of birth from the hospital records to the Pre-School health module.

The information given by a woman who is in hospital to have a baby, is given for the sole purpose of her care and the care of her child, unless she gives explicit permission for it to be used in other ways.

This transfer of information from one system to another without the knowledge or consent of the person concerned is a clear breach of the early Younger Principle. In April 1978 the BMA representatives on the CHCC, in despair that the other members of the CHCC were paying only lip service to the need for confidentiality, discussed the problem with the BMA's Central Ethical Committee (CEC)

Following an emergency meeting at which the CGCC's proposals were examined, the CEC warned doctors that if they were to take part in such a scheme they would be behaving unethically and they would risk appearing before the General Medical Council, the medical profession's disciplinary organisation.

The next day the CHCC met and agreed three principles put forward by the CEC and subsequently reiterated by Mr Roland Moyle in reply to a Parliamentary Question (Hansard 26/5/78 col 809)

1. Identifiable information is to be regarded as held for the specific purpose of the continuing care of the patient (parent or guardian in the case of a child) and not for any other purposes.

2. Access to identifiable information held in medical records is to be confined to the author and to the person clinically responsible for the patient during the episode from which the data has been collected (or their successors) unless specifically authorised by the clinician in the clinical interest of the patients.

3. An individual is not to be identifiable from data supplied for statistical or research purposes except when follow-up of the individual patient is a necessary part of the research (and either the patient has given informed prior consent or consent has been obtained from the Chairman of an appropriate ethical committee).

Despite agreeing these principles the CHCC did nothing to modify their system proposals to fulfil the ethical principles it had accepted.

Most recently the BMA Annual Representative Meeting resolved that Government be required to introduce adequate legislative safeguards before the implementation of any new computer scheme for the storage of medical information.

Extended Confidence

There is no doubt that the ethical precepts stated by Hippocrates 2,500 years ago were strictly adhered to by doctors at least until 1948. Many GPs still believe literally that 'Whatever in connection with my professional practice or not in connection with it I see or hear in the life of men which ought not to be spoken abroad I will not divulge as reckoning that all such should be kept secret'.

A hospital consultant pædiatrician was heard to say recently that 'in the context of day to day practice in a District General Hospital, everything in the General Medical Council's book on Professional Conduct about confidentiality isn't worth the paper it's written on'. Quite a contrast. Two diametrically opposed views, neither to be discounted as emanating from eccentric individuals or groups.

The real cause of these polarised views is the rise, in hospital medicine, of the multi-disciplinary approach to health care. Consultants have, through overwork, lack of foresight, or a vague belief that a loss of confidentiality was outweighed by the medical gain to the patient, allowed other groups of staff to have access to their medical records about their patients.

Obviously the situation varies from one hospital to another. In some, only doctors and their secretaries see the patient's notes. In others, they are available to social workers, pharmacists, occupational therapists, laboratory staff and students in any or all of these disciplines.

In Oxfordshire, consultants have experienced problems at case conferences about children which are also attended by police officers. Is it right for a doctor to co-operate with a case conference where he will, of necessity, divulge information given to him in confidence to people whose responsibility is clearly not to the person who is the subject of the case conference but to a superior officer? Probably not, unless he has the patients' or the guardians' consent. If a doctor feels that there is sufficient danger to a child from the parents that he must involve an outside agency then he should inform the parents of the action he proposes to take, despite the damage such action may do to his relationship with the family.

The relationship will probably suffer less from honesty than from underhandedness with the attendant suspicion and anxiety.

Advances in Semi-Conductor Technology

The transistor and the stored program digital computer both appeared about the time of the creation of the National Health Service. The awe with which the developers of the first computer regarded their kilowatt consuming child is illustrated by their belief that four computers would be sufficient for the world's needs.

Transistor integrated circuits were developed by Fairchild in 1959 and in 1964 Gordon Moore predicted that the complexity of integrated circuits, in terms of the number of elements on each chip, would continue to double each year. To date, with circuits containing 2^{18} elements now available, Gordon Moore's prediction is running true.

At the same time, the cost of elements in a computer — and memory elements seem to be a good standard for comparison — has decreased dramatically. In 1975 ferrite core store cost approximately the same as metal oxide semi-conductor memory (0.25 - 0.5 cent/bit). The relative change in memory prices and the current figures for this year for dynamic MOS memory, would be a figure of approximately 0.05 cent/bit or lower.

Two relevant examples of software advances are MICKIE, a microprocessor-based patient interviewing system presently undergoing DHSS trials in Fulham and the West Middlesex Hospital after development at the National Physical Laboratory, and the highly successful Exeter Community Health Services Computer Project at Exeter.

The Exeter project is based on an ICL 1904A with 128K core store and front end 7903 communications processor. At present VDUs provide real time processing for GP systems and with some terminals in the Royal Devon and Exeter Hospital, these are the only systems run in real time. There is a fast line to each surgery and a line sharing adaptor servicing the VDUs. A separate slow line is provided for the surgery Termiprinter.

Analysis of patient records are done at an author's request by batch processing and output on a lineprinter.

Summing Up

In the last few months a number of conclusions have emerged from this debate:

1 .Confidentiality belongs to the patient. It is not the doctor's job to classify (as is done in Sweden) a patient's information into various categories of sensitivity: details of contraceptive treatment may only be of 'medium-grade' sensitivity for most people, but keeping them secret may be of the highest importance to a Catholic woman, married or unmarried.

2 . The superficial slide away from orthodox standards of confidentiality, among some hospital doctors in particular, is not acceptable to the great majority of the profession when they are made to consider the problem. Absolute personal privacy is incompatible with a multi-disciplinary approach to medical care and this dilemma is unresolved at the moment. From the support we have received in our dispute with the CHCC, we know that patients wish to be able to consult their doctors with an assurance of privacy.

3 . Ten or twelve years ago the technology of computing was at a level that would have made record storage systems, of the size and nature envisaged by the CHCC and operated by the Exeter Computer Project, impossible on any but a batch processing basis. There have occurred such massive changes in technology that the Exeter system, conceived in 1971 and operational in 1973, has achieved clinical record storage and retrieval within an ethically acceptable operating framework, and that there is no excuse for a failure to incorporate adequate conditions and standards of confidentiality in any new system. It is probable that the Exeter system itself could be altered to put the same facilities into GP's surgeries, with even greater control in the hands of a doctor. Doctors should be identifiably responsible to the patient for the confidentiality and security of the information that they gather in the course of their work. Peer or hierarchical groups of small computers allied to portable peripheral devices can provide most of the facilities in the Exeter system.

4.3   Report from the Workshop on Social Work and Medical Reports

Ron Lacey

I have some considerable difficulty in giving the report from our workshop. When I tell you that in the workshop we had four doctors and four representatives from consumer organisations, you will understand that we very soon threw away the ball and got on with the game!

One of the points that was made very early was that, as far as medical records were concerned, the best guarantee for confidentiality was doctors' handwriting. I would add that that point was made by a doctor.

Our workshop did not really address itself very much to the issue of computers, or indeed very much in terms of the control of information. The workshop spent most of its time in very vigorous discussion about client or patient access to records. This was something that the consumer organisation representatives on the one hand had very strong views on, and I think the medical representatives in the workshop also.

A number of points were made by either side. There was, of course, the reference to the need for research and computer use in research for epidemiological studies etc. Amongst the doctors there were some who felt that it would be reasonable for patients to have access to some records. There were points where medical and social work records were treated rather similarly. A case was put that there was not an automatic case for access to records on the part of patients or clients, because records may contain information about other members of the family. An example was given of a wife seeking medical help with perhaps a venereal desease which was contracted outside the marriage, and the problems which would there ensue. As far as social work records are concerned, we were concerned about the situation of a child in care and notes about a parent or a foster parent on that child's case file, which perhaps the child or the parent of the child should not automatically have access to.

The other point that was made specifically in relation to computer records, was that computers may in fact improve the situation in some ways as far as social work records are concerned because of the difficulty of codifying subjective information. The point was also made that the access to computer records would be, by and large, not very useful, because the meat of the material was in manual systems. And manual systems very much preoccupied the group.

There was reference to a case which was discussed on the Esther Rantzen programme where a patient was seeking to take litigation against a doctor for operating on the wrong finger, and the problems which ensued in that case about getting the evidence in order to get the legal aid. The fact that a mistake had been made in that case came to light by accident in discussion between the patient and her GP.

Running right through our workshop was our concern about manual rather than computer records.

A number of points were put on the side of non-disclosure of a patient's case notes. The point was made that often the case notes may represent *aides mémoire* to the doctor rather than a specific diagnosis, or notes to colleagues about a particular patient. The question was asked several times as to what the benefit was of non-disclosure of records. I do not think any answer emerged on either side from that. Again, one of the members of the workshop referred to a previous conference, where a nurse was describing how she would feel if she would want to know what a social worker might be writing about her, but would not want the social worker to know what she (the nurse) may be writing about the social worker!

At MIND we are particularly concerned, of course, about psychiatric records and their potential for harm for people in the long term. If I can give you an example of the sort of case that comes to us: last year we were contacted by a lady in Exeter who some 20 years ago, had psychiatric treatment for depression. She had had 10 days' treatment, come out, resumed her life and remained in stable employment for the ensuing 22 years. She then applied for a job in a local hospital and was turned down on the grounds that she would not be able to handle the stress of the job. This decision had been based on the fact that she had had psychiatric treatment some 22 years previously.

I think that is as far as I can take our report.

Section 5

Police and National Security Records

5.1 A Summary of Developments

Tony Bunyan, Director, State Research

Introduction

The application of technology to police record-keeping is a comparatively recent development. It was only in the 1950s that a concerted attempt was made to rationalise the storage of information about crime and criminals. Prior to this, the manual Criminal Records Office (CRO) at Scotland Yard was the only source for inquiries outside of the local police forces. What is important to note about policing in Britain from 1829 (when the first modern force was created) up to the early 1960s, is that the information held was almost exclusively concerned with the *convicted* criminal.

What distinguishes the period since the 1960s is the introduction of pre-emptive policing. This involves two assumptions:

first: that those convicted of a crime are likely to commit another criminal act and,

second: that the police have to keep themselves informed about those people who are *likely* to commit crimes.

It is certainly true that much information on 'suspected' criminals has always been available in the informal sense, either in the head of an officer or in their notebooks. However, it is the formalisation and centralisation of information over the past decade which has marked a qualitative change in British policing. Furthermore, the assumption of guilt which underlies these changes clearly offends against the traditional rule of law that presupposes innocence until guilt is proven.

National security records, that is those held by the security and intelligence agencies, present a problem of quite a different order. If little is known about police record-keeping, then virtually nothing is known about the records of the Special Branch or MI5. In addition, most of the several million people held on file by these agencies are not guilty of any offence in the criminal sense, but have fallen within the perview of these agencies because they are considered to be 'subversives' or 'security risks'.

Police Records

Police records on convicted and 'suspected' criminals are now held at local, regional and national level. The first development towards centralisation was the creation of the Regional Criminal Records Offices in 1964. The second was the government's decision in 1969 to give its approval for the creation of a national computer system which was to hold all criminal records and thus to make this information available swiftly to local forces. This computer, called the Police National Computer Unit (PCNU), is now in operation and holds 3.8 million records on convicted persons, 250,000 on stolen vehicles, the index to 2.25 million fingerprints, and 60,000 wanted and missing persons. All of these categories are, by and large, unexceptional.

However, this national computer also holds records on 19 million vehicle owners in this country. The police claim that this information helps in their work to prevent crime. This may well be true, but does it justify holding information on the majority of the adult population who have never been convicted of any criminal act?

What is even more disturbing is that there is space on the computer for additional information to be recorded about vehicle owners under one of three headings (SUS: temporary suspicion of being used in a crime; POL: being used for police purposes; INT: of long-term interest to the police). In one recent case the information recorded related to a person's political associations (the Hunt Saboteurs Association), and this practice was confirmed by a Home Office Minister (Hansard, 2.12.77).

The other area of police record-keeping related to 'suspected' criminals, represents another highly questionable practice, and much of this information is held on the Metropolitan Police National Intelligence

Computer. This computer holds 'intelligence' gathered by the Fraud Squad and the Serious Crimes Squad on the one hand, and on 'suspected' illegal immigrants, 'suspected' drug-takers and dealers, and selected Special Branch 'suspects' on the other.

The Home Office, in announcing the formation of two of these units, those covering suspected illegal immigrants and drugs, made their pre-emptive function explicit. The purpose of the units they said 'would be to receive, collate, evaluate and disseminate information relating to known or *suspected* offenders' (Home Office press release 4.10.72).

The Lindop Committee was denied access to information about this computer by the Metropolitan Police — a decision which the Home Office backed. The Committee erroneously thought the computer only held information related to London and therefore were unaware of its national function. However, the Committee did express disquiet over the multi-feature retrieval capability of the computer.

Another computer programme started by the Thames Valley police force in 1974 represents a major step in the extension of pre-emptive policing records to the local force level. This programme is based on the information gathered by police 'collators' whose job is to gather 'intelligence'. This 'intelligence' covers criminal names, vehicles, crimes, and occurrences.

While computerisation in itself does not represent a threat to privacy of the individual and civil liberties, the centralisation and access to information on large sectors of the population (who have no opportunity to question the accuracy of the information held) certainly does.

When the creation of PNCU was announced '*Police Review*' remarked that it: 'is to be far more comprehensive than any other computerised intelligence service in the world' (5.5.72), and went on to describe this general development in policing:

> 'Police intelligence is now forward-looking, anticipating who is going to commit what, when and where, and because it is so purposeful it is also frequently libellous ....
> Much of the information is personal details of a suspect, his family associates, way of life and although it may seem to trespass on the freedom of the individual it is the bread and butter of successful policemanship.'

National Security Records

It is arguable that the records held by the security and intelligence agencies in this country represent an even greater threat to civil liberties because these agencies are not accountable, nor were they created, by democratic institutions. Very broadly the records they keep — which run into several millions — fall into three categories:—

i) those suspected of being foreign espionage agents in the direct or indirect (but conscious) employment of a foreign power;

ii) those employed by the state or in key industries who work on 'sensitive' areas; and leading business people, MPs, and the media;

iii) those considered to be 'subversives' by the agencies

It is the second and third of these categories which are of concern in the context of this conference.

Very little information has become available over the past 20 years on the extent of 'vetting' carried out in government departments and of workers in industry considered to be working on 'sensitive' areas of production. The 'vetting' of an employee is carried out without his/her knowledge and with no opportunity to correct the information placed on file about them. An adverse report can lead to loss of promotion prospects, failure to employ in the first instance, and failure to move successfully between departments or industries. What is becoming apparent is that there has been a resurgence of 'vetting' which is causing concern to the major civil service unions.

The third category is of equal concern, in the light of two connected developments. The first is the now admitted growth of the Special Branch, the political arm of the police, since the early 1960s from 300 officers to nearly 2,000 in 1979. The second is the redefinition of the scope of their work (and of MI5, the undercover internal security agency) in the 1970s. This centres around the concept of 'subversion'. In 1963 Lord Denning, in his report on the Profumo affair, spelt out the official definition of 'subversion' as those who 'would contemplate the *overthrow* of government by *unlawful* means' (para 230 CMND 2152, 1963).

However, in April 1978, Mr. Rees the Home Secretary confirmed an earlier statement by Lord Harris that the current definition of 'subversion' (and therefore the scope of the Special Branch and MI5 activities) was as follows:

'those activities which threaten the safety or wellbeing of the State, and are intended to *undermine* or *overthrow* parliamentary democracy by *political, industrial* or violent means' (Hansard 6.4.78. My emphasis).

While Lord Denning's definition is capable of clear interpretation under statute and common law, i.e. 'unlawful means', Mr. Rees' is in no way restricted to unlawful activities. Indeed it can be taken to mean all political and trade union activity which, in the eyes of the security agencies, represents a threat to the state.

If the national security records held by these state agencies are based on the above presumption, then there is a clear need for democratic accountability and statutory controls over their actions. And the widely-held presumption that questions of 'national security' are 'above' political debate represents a very grave threat to political and civil rights, unless this presumption can be effectively demolished.

5.2 Report from the Workshop on Police and National Security Records

Peter Ashman,
Assistant Secretary, JUSTICE.

Since the people who attended this workshop consisted of lawyers, senior police officers, civil libertarians, politicians, journalists and other interested parties, it is not surprising perhaps that there was very little agreement indeed on any of the issues that were raised.

Specifically, we disagreed on whether there was any need for control of police and national security records, and if there was, what sort of material should be controlled and who finally should control it? On one hand, it was argued that there has been a qualitative change in the content of police records in recent years. Formerly there had only been hard, factual data or convictions, whereas, since about the 1960s, there had been the gathering of intelligence information on suspicious activity and suspected criminals. This is known generically as pre-emptive policing. It was argued that there was in fact no control over what was recorded. Perhaps the only limits to this sort of data was the physical capacity of the recording devices themselves. Nor was there adequate control over the use of this material.

Against this, it was argued that what was on the files today, was really no different from what had existed in the old beat books of local bobbies. Society and criminals had become more mobile and police information had to become more mobile too. The police could not effectively prevent or solve crime with one eye blinded, so to speak. Moreover, the suspicion of criminal or subversive activity did not confer in itself any disability on the suspected person. Information would only come out in court, and if it was wrong it would be rebutted in court. And if any damage ensued from misinformation or misuse of information, there were adequate remedies in civil and criminal law to correct this. The police were subject to administrative and legal controls and the Official Secrets Act, and they were fully accountable for what they did with the material.

It was pointed out, however, that this sort of argument only pertained to the correction of the misuse of information. It did not prevent it. An example was given of someone whose house was raided for bomb materials, because he was suspected of being an anarchist, and the embarrassment and distress and damage that was caused could not really be adequately compensated for in civil and criminal remedies.

There was also a good deal of disagreement on the content and the availability of records. Some people felt that all the police and the national security records should be available to the data subjects, regardless of content, and that there should be adequate opportunity to correct misinformation. Some members also doubted whether certain material should exist at all on these records, such as one's political activity, one's personal associates or one' religious beliefs.

On the other hand, it was argued that it was quite impossible to preclude the gathering or storing of any information, because there was no knowing when this sort of information would become relevant and valuable. Perhaps examples of this could be sectarian animosity amongst ethnic groups in the population, or a particular crime affecting a particular minority. An example perhaps here would be information about some-one's homosexuality. If there was murder going on amongst homosexuals, it would be both for the benefit of the homosexual and for the apprehension of the criminal that the police knew about this sort of information.

Moreover, it was argued that the free information of intelligence material to data subjects would assist criminals in the furtherance of crime, because they would be able to go along and find out who could be safely used for drug trafficking or illegal immigration and who was suspected. Also, it was argued that it was no good just having police and national security files open. If there was going to be openness, all the files of all organisations ought to be opened, and then the police and the security people would have no need to gather this sort of information. Against this was argued that, since the police records were the ones most capable of causing damage and distress, these were the ones that it was most important to have open. You can see that there was really no agreement!

Most people did feel, however, that there was scope for the DPA to draw up a code of practice with the police, laying down general guidelines which the DPA could supervise. But — and we are thinking here particularly of intelligence records — because this information would be very sensitive, perhaps the investigation of complaints would have to be done *in camera*. Virtually everyone agreed that the police should not be allowed to give the information which they have — particularly intelligence information — to groups outside the police forces, except perhaps for national security reasons and to courts.

Overall, it was recognised that one had to strike a balance between the legitimate desires of an individual to protection against misinformation and the misuse of information, and the equally legitimate expectations of members of society that they should be adequately protected against criminal activity. And, of course, very often it was the same people in both cases: even if you had misinformation about you on the files, you still wanted to be protected from being hit over the head! It was felt that there would have to be a lot more discussion inside and outside Parliament where this balance lay.

Inevitably, most of our discussion centred on police records, not least because there is very little information about the content of national security records or their collection — although it was recognised that most of the arguments and the issues are the same in both cases.

There were four groups under surveillance:

a. Those suspected of espionage in the ultimate employ of a foreign power.

b. Those suspected of terrorism.

c. Those employed by the State in sensitive areas, MPs, leading businessmen and those in the media.

d. Those considered subversive, using the definition of subversion adopted by Merlyn Rees in April 1978 and quoted in Tony Bunyan's paper.

Some members saw a distinction between groups (a) and (b), surveillance of whom is necessary, and groups (c) and (d), surveillance of whom constituted a grave threat to civil liberty.

There was disagreement on the type of activity which required surveillance. Some felt that there was considerable and unjustified invasion of privacy in undisclosed vetting of people, which could lead to their loss of jobs. Others objected on civil liberties grounds to the vetting of political and industrial activists, since this sort of activity was both normal and proper in any democratic society.

On the other hand, the Home Secretary's definition of 'subversion' is the overthrowing or the undermining of parliamentary democracy by political or industrial activity, and many people felt that, in our sort of society, it was unlikely that parliamentary democracy would be overthrown by violent means — which were the other ones mentioned — and that if it was going to be overthrown it would be by political or industrial activity. Therefore, it was quite right and proper to place under surveillance people engaged in this sort of activity.

The only real agreement which we had on national security records was, in fact, the inadequacy of the DPC proposals. It was felt that, whoever was chosen to supervise the national security records, would be hamstrung by the need to maintain secrecy, and that one person alone could not expect to be long regarded as objective or independent, either by data subjects or by data users. It was felt that, inevitably, such a person would attract allegations of being the creature of one side or the other after a period of time and that this just was not good enough. It was felt that either there must be greater independent control — perhaps all the members of the DPA — or the existing Parliamentary controls would have to continue, but perhaps Parliament could usefully drop the convention that ministers can avoid answering questions on the grounds of national security.

The wide divergence of our views, although it did not lead to any uniformity of recommendation, did lead to a full change of information, attitudes and opinions on the subject. If any consensus is to be reached on these very important questions, there is going to have to be a lot more discussion in order that the conflicting interests can be resolved.

Section 6

The Information Explosion

John McNulty, Managing Director, General Robots

The old definition of a computer used to be 'a machine which was capable of storing a number of instructions and then executing them'. I think that was the conventional wisdom that used to be. My definition of a computer — or the most active constituent part of a computer — is 'a switch'. A computer operates by a series of switches. It holds all its memory, all its data, in these banks you have been talking about. It holds data in there by means of switching in ones or zeros or negative or positive voltages or high or low voltages, and I think you can reduce most of it to switching. The reason I have simplified it to such a great extent is that a lot of people get terribly frightened about computers. In the fifties, if you remember, you used to see in comics and popular newspapers, if anything was being described as specially super it was 'atomic'. Now it is a computer, and people either regard it with awe or with terror — or possibly they invest too much hope in it.

It is a very simple beast, the computer. Although the original ones were very big and steaming and full of all sorts of strange clanky pieces, we have now got them down to very tiny sizes.

The fact remains that the original computers actually used relays and bits out of telephone exchanges and so on, because, really, what you are doing with a computer is switching. You may hold data in there, but you are switching odd bits up and down and then having a look to see which position those switches are in. A programme itself is also a series of — if you like — switches. You go through a sequence. The other thing you need is a clock. A purist would argue that a clock can be regarded as a series of switches as well.

Why do I reduce it to such fundamental elements? Because I am going to put it to you that there is already a multinational, international, massive information network which we use every day. I refer to the telephone network. Although we do not think of the telephone as anything to do with computers, it is in fact an information handling device. None of you ever think in your wildest dreams about all the nasty things that are going on inside various strange buildings around London, mangling up your voice and packaging it up and sending it elsewhere. But there is an awful lot of processing going on. In the main your voice does not get chopped about too much at the moment. It is simply routed. But a lot of information in computers is not so much operated on — i.e. arithmetical operations — but is simply routed from one file to another, or it is changed in its format or we add up how many people are left-handed and were born on Wednesday, but basically we are not manipulating arithmetic operations other than counting a number of records. What we are really doing is switching it around — messaging it. It is sometimes known as data message. The famous word 'processing' which you will all have heard of is also a case of messaging information. You are not really doing too much numerically to it except saying 'how many pages have you got?' 'how many words?' — something like that, remembering where you are.

The telephone network has been around for a very long time. It is once again in the news on the subject of privacy and access. Is there anybody listening in? There always is a chance of somebody listening in, either officially or unofficially, by design or by accident.

Reading through the papers for this conference, I have a suspicion that there has not been too much emphasis on communications — tele-communication, distant communications. About 1974-75, taking the total volume of international telecommunications traffic going out and into this country, the amount of data going out exceeded the amount of voice traffic. And it is going on. There is a lot of data whizzing around on the networks.

Where is it all going? Where is it all coming from? What are people doing with it? We do not really know. But to think in terms of punch cards and magnetic drums and files of tape and all the rest of it is all very well, but you may be leading yourself up a garden path. The computer industry, until fairly recently, believed that telecommunications — or the communications industry — was one industry, and the computer industry was another industry. What we are finding more and more every day is that, of course, it was an artificial distinction, which is why I insist on that definition of a computer being composed of switches, and therefore, rightfully, finding its place in the hierarchy of telecommunications-type technology.

What has that got to do with privacy and data banks? I will give you a particular example. Lloyds Bank instituted a thing called 'Cashpoint'. I think they were the first people to have a truly on-line system. You run along to the outside of the bank, poke a bit of plastic in and the door opens and you press some keys and money spits out. I have always been waiting to see somebody have tons of money come out, but it has not happened yet. However, they did the first actual on-line system; that is, that they actually checked in your account to make sure you had some lolly in there. Prior to that the other systems were a sort of luncheon voucher-type system. You have a little ticket, but they already know that you have paid for it effectively, so when you poke it in you get some money out, but there is no on-line interaction and it has not actually looked at your data bank.

Lloyds, being very responsible and proper and also concerned about people not running off with barrowloads of cash from outside the place, wanted to make sure that the data was encoded and encrypted — scrambled. So they wrote an algorithm programme to unscramble this coded data so that people can fool around with it, tap into it and all the rest of it. It is a sensible precaution, and they put this to the Post Office. And the Post Office, who have a total monopoly on telecommunications in this country said, 'Ah, well, if you send data, it is legal, but if you send messages over a computer network, it is illegal'. Information if it is messages, is different from information if it is data. I cannot see the difference between data and data myself. Nonetheless, there we are.

As a result they said, 'We want to know whether you are sending messages down those lines. You could be sending 'Hello Fred, how are you?' instead of 'X1234'. They said, 'Let us have the encryption algorithm. We will keep it safe for you.' The idea of somebody outside Lloyds having the encryption algorithm so that they can tap into lines to make sure that Lloyds are not sending naughty old human-type messages rather than computer-type messages, raises a few questions. There was a great furore about it, and I am not quite sure how it was settled. I think all parties concerned were highly embarrassed and tried to keep it quiet, but nonetheless, it does raise a point, does it not? People accessing data.

You are familiar with telephone taps. You get crossed lines every other day. One should always assume that the telephone is never a secure device. But I go on-line to computers a lot. And quite often if you dial up, you can find that your port drops occasionally and a whole scribble comes up on the screen. You pick up the phone and it's 'Ello, I'm trying to get Fred's Garage but there's this whistle on the line' and you put it back and somebody has dialled across. Occasionally what happens is that your port drops on the computer and you drop back in again. And there you are, on somebody else's account number — they all have account numbers to get in and a logging code and a password, it is very secure — there you are in somebody else's file!

There has not been too much discussion about that. It has happened randomly so far. I do not think that there is anybody deliberately tapping into data lines anywhere. I want to try to set the new technology. It may come as a surprise to some of the techno-maniacal amongst us that the information age is not new. It is, if not quite as old as the hills, older than the Pyramids or Stonehenge. Information is a vital part of *homo sapiens* — information, no *sapiens* — or, more to the point — no *sapiens*, no information.

I will give you my own definition of civilisation. Civilisation is software. We work on it in our heads. The Information Age is something we and countless generations before us have dealt with every day of our lives. To say the Information Age is upon us now is nonsense. Our ability to move and manipulate information has accelerated steadily, and we now find ourselves with a dizzying number of choices as we actually approach the speed of light. We do not have to enter the regions of science fiction when we are quite literally dealing with information travelling at the speed of light. It is here today, and we have to come to terms with it today or be left behind like the members of some superstitious tribe cowering in abject terror at the very notion of having to think as rational individuals

The Information Age is the Age of Man. It is the sheer speed of electronic communications which has nudged us into the dim realisation that change is upon us at a new rate and in a new way. Electronic communications have been with us for quite sometime. Have we been ignoring them in the hope that they will go away?

Initially, it did happen — and this is a salutory case. Back in the 1880s, when Alexander Graham Bell came over to show the Postmaster General the Bell telephone, it was rejected. The Postmaster said that he could see no use for the telephone since the GPO already had a very find telegram service. In any case, if someone was foolish enough to buy a telephone, what use would it be since he would have no-one to call up? Irrefutable logic!

We cannot ignore electronic communications, not only because we cannot afford to ignore it financially, when it costs dramatically less to move information than it does to move goods or people; but also because the evolution of civilisation is reaching the beginnings of a new renaissance. We are only at the beginning of an amplification of man's mind, which promises to take us further than any science fiction prophet has ever dreamed. Man may even begin to have the courage to face himself and come to terms with the ultimate information processor, his mind.

On a mundane and mondial level, we all work and trade with information. We even carry it around in our pockets. No, I do not mean a microfilmed copy of the Encyclopaedia Britannica or even a little black book with useful phone numbers in it. I am talking about money. What is money? Commodities are ultimately paid for, not by money, but by other commodities, and money is merely the commonly used medium of exchange. It plays only an intermediary role. What the seller wants ultimately to receive in exchange for the commodities sold, is other commodities. Every commodity produced is therefore a price, as it were, for other commodities produced.

Money is a tool of exchange which cannot exist unless there are goods produced and men able to produce them. Money is the material shape of the principle that men who wish to deal with one another must deal by trade and give value for value. Money is a specially coded form of information. We all carry little promises around in our pockets and we even write promises — cheques — to pay promises — to other people. All these bits of paper, worthless metal and plastic are specialised forms of information. To facilitate trading and information exchange on a global scale we need to be able to move money electronically, not mechanically. And at this point we find ourselves trying to stuff banknotes down the telephone.

People in the USA are trying to move money around. It is known as electronic funds transfer. Because we have a slightly different banking system over here it has not become such a significant point over here, but it is going to be a highly significant point because you are going to have files on people's creditworthiness and all the rest of it. It is there. It is there in the States. There are numerous banking laws about inter-state trading and so on which are sometimes quite ludicrous. Is a cash dispenser a branch, and is a branch a cash dispenser? Is a computer terminal a bank? They are finding those problems because they have not redefined their objectives; they have not thought around the problem sufficiently and thought what they are dealing with.

What I am worried about is people thinking to themselves, 'Yes, well, computers are big things that sit in the basement and we feed punch cards into them and we can lock the computer room. Great! Nobody gets in or out! Fantastic! We review the data regularly,' and all the rest. Computers are changing very rapidly. I get two or three brand new developments — I am not talking about products, I am talking about state-of-the-art changes — which land on my desk every week — two or three completely new state-of-the-art changes. What does that mean? It means new products later on. It means changes in the way we handle information. It means that this dreaded microprocessor which you are thinking about in the future is actually here, doing things now. It means, for example, that I have got a little case down there with a terminal in it. It is made by Texas Instruments — alpha keyboard, thermal printer — wonder of modern technology. It has one, if not two, micro-processors in it. It also has 20,000 characters storage, non-volatile — that means it will not go away when I pull the plug out — bubble memory, expendable up to 80,000 characters. That is a bit boring now, it is established. It means I can carry a data base in and out of this room. You would not know, would you? I could have facts and figures on every single person in this room in that case. Have I?

All these micros that everybody is going to have in their own home, doing all these wonderful things, are not much use unless they connect to other things. They are going to have telephone lines coming into them, one way or another, regardless of which way the Post Office handle it. They are going to be inter-connected. That means that — back to the medical records situation — we can see a doctor having patient records in his own local floppy disc. In fact, there are doctors now with them. He has got his own local file. I suppose you could put in a security situation so that only decanted statistical information was released to the big network, and the local personal information was kept in the floppy discs and he could put them into his briefcase and take them home with him at the end of the day in the same way as he keeps a card index today.

I can tell you categorically that I can gain access to virtually any data bank, given enough time and money. Categorically! The system is extremely leaky. You should think about data banks as being a big filing cabinet. A lot of information is dynamic and floating around. The next logical development in satellite technology will probably mean that, because computers are getting very fast and very small, we will start putting computers up there. It is a very good environment for them. At the moment most of the satellites are a bit stupid. All they can do is relay stuff. But they might do a little bit of at least store and forward. Store and forward is where you are trying to get a Telex or a message to somebody and, because their line or their machine is not free, it is poked in centrally and held waiting until there is a spare slot and then it is sent over. Is that a data bank? it is very dynamic. It is only held there for an hour or so, maybe three hours. But maybe the system goes down. Maybe they have a tape or disc back-up or bubble memory storage there at the centre in case their system goes down so that they can keep those records. So the messages that are going to and fro, are also capable of being stored at the centre, even though they are being offically transmitted from point to point. We are going to have more and more data store and forward. That means that our satellites are going to become more intelligent; they are going to have computing capabilities.

Computers and telecommunications cannot be divided. It has been an artificial divide, as we are now rapidly discovering in the industry, and in the future it is going to be extremely difficult to differentiate between data and data and data. What do I mean by that? I mean printed words and the Telex network, which will be handled as streams of binary information. I mean voice data, which will be voices that are translated into bits with things called pulse code modulation devices, so that you will have streams of bits floating around which are Telex, and streams of bits floating around which are true data because they go into the old-fashioned chug-chug, steam-driven computers. It is all going to be streams of bits — data. If you think you are going to be able to differentiate between it, and if you think you are going to be able to have some kind of control mechanism monitoring all that, I think you are very mistaken. There are just torrents and torrents of information being flung around the globe now, and we have not the faintest idea what is in there. By the time we start poking satellites up there with some storage capability, who is going to go up there and inspect that? And would they let him hitch a ride on the shuttle?

I have reserved some time for questions, so if anybody wants to know how to access a data base in three easy steps or tap a telephone line, I will tell them.

Question:

You have not mentioned the subject of privacy in the sense that you have not said whether there could be any controls at all. You have suggested that the Lindop Committee and all of us here are wasting our time, because there would be no way that we could get any control.

Mr. McNulty: Did I say that?

Questioner:

No, but the indication is there. Is that a correct assessment of your view? Could you give any idea of what controls could be possible, given the expansion of computers and telecommunications the way you describe?

Mr. McNulty:

It is jolly difficult. That is what I was trying to get across to you all. I am not saying you are wasting your time, but I am saying that you are waking up to computers and computers are waking up to telecommunications.

You have got to do an awful lot of running to stay ahead of the field. It is tremendously difficult. More than 50 per cent of the traffic on international lines is now data and the rest of it is voice.

Questioner:

Should there be controls, or do you think there is no need for controls?

Mr. McNulty:

I do not like the idea of people holding information on me which may be incorrect, anymore than anybody else does. But we have got some serious thinking to do — very serious — and there is an awful lot of data there.

Question:

Can I just comment on one thing you have been saying about the difficulty of distinguishing between different types of data. A thing which has worried me at times is this. It is nice when people talk about transnational, transborder data flow and so on, and I think — as you have really said — that it is going to be impossible to know what it is. I do not like the idea of having any law where I know for a start that I have no way whatever of enforcing it. At the moment — sure, you say that more than half of the data flowing between countries and over the telephone is computer data. But actually, because of the way the telephone system works, it is converted into voice data. So there is no way of distinguishing that from speech between people. In a few years time the telephone exchanges are going to be computers, and the voice communication will be converted into digital pulses and there will be no way of distinguishing me telephoning my cousin in America or me accessing a computer in America. The only way of distinguishing is censoring, and saying that none of this is allowed to happen. It is the difficulty of distinguishing between the container and the content. I know at the moment, for example, that the law says I must not send pornographic literature by post. How do they know, without actually opening every letter? It is really a matter of saying 'if you are caught doing it I can do something, but I have no way of checking that it does not happen all the time'.

Mr. McNulty: Absolutely.

Question:

Can I raise a point? You said that, given enough time and money, you could get into any data base. You are not saying anything new. Given enough time and money, I could get into the Bank of England to steal the gold, if they have any left. The distinction is that you make your computer whether it happens to be carried in a little box like that, and I have got to get hold of the thing first, before I can get into it. And if you do not plug it in, there is no way I can get access to the information you hold. If you write encrypted software for it, complicated algorithms — fine! With time and money I could get in. Without time and without money, and if you changed your software every week, I could not get in. It is exactly the same situation as the standard bricks-and-mortar security which we have round our filing cabinets.

Mr. McNulty:

My knowledge is that you are going to have to move it in and out if you are going to trade, deal with the rest of the outside world. Going back to your original question, there is a ray of hope — I do not want to panic everybody. There are certain algorithms coming — Professor Samet is far better qualified than I to judge on them — called 'trapdoor function' algorithms — a new form of encryption which is causing lots of dispute in the States at the moment. Theoretically, it may be possible to do a one-way mathematical transformation which will make it possible for you locally to code up your own data before you poke it down the line, and other people cannot get at it. You will have private and public messages. Maybe that is the answer. But my old feeling is that — apart from this trapdoor function which I am not sure about, and no other mathematician I have spoken to seems to know about it properly yet — we might be able to code things up uniquely, but the indications are that if you can code something it can be uncoded. I know for a fact, if you try to go on-line in Russia, they have a very simple way of dealing with it. If you are dialling up with a terminal, just to prove that the lines are monitored, if they hear a whistle on that line it is out, because they think it might be encrypted stuff, I assume. I know this because we have had people over there demonstrating on-line equipment and the line is cut after a few seconds, as soon as a data tone appears.

Questioner:

But you can send coded messages in clear. It does not have to be visibly coded.

Mr. McNulty: No, quite.

Chairman:

If I can leave you with this final thought: I have always considered that one of the biggest safeguards against Big Brother before the advent of the computer, was the impossibility of having enough police or security agents to monitor everything that a population of, say, 50 million people were doing and saying at any one moment, and I think it is very comforting that the flow of data across borders and within a country is increasing to such an extend that the amount of it would be too astronomical for the most ardent Big Brother that one can imagine to monitor the whole of that traffic. I think that is a pretty good safeguard.

Section 7
THE INTERNATIONAL PERSPECTIVE

7.1. Developments within OECD and its Member Countries

Russell Pipe,
Editor, Transnational Data Report

We should start by taking note of what is going on internationally in this data protection privacy field. We have eight countries which have national laws — Austria, Canada, Denmark, France, Germany, Norway, Sweden and the United States. All but the United States and Canadian laws are omnibus laws covering the private sector as well as central government and other government institutions. During this year of 1979 it appears reasonably certain that there will be four or five additional countries to adopt broad-scope data protection laws. They are Belgium, Luxembourg, Netherlands and Spain.

There are two countries which have put data protection into their constitutions in the last two years, indeed have added references to personal information and computerised information. One of them is Portugal and the other is Spain. So, in a sense, and as I understand it from the Portugese, they feel that this constitutional provision initially qualified them as having indeed even a higher protection than national laws passed by their Parliament.

In addition to these countries, numbering some fourteen or fifteen, there are five other countries well advanced in this area who are planning to adopt such legislation. When you take the OECD area — which is actually 23 countries plus Yugoslavia as an associate member, these being the so-called free western democracies barring a few which are not members, together with countries such as Japan, Australia, New Zealand, Canada and the United States — they comprise all but one or two countries such as Greece and Turkey, which have not yet sorted this issue out too clearly, but which also plan to have such legislation. And when you add the member states of the Council of Europe — of which I believe there are five non-members of OECD — there are some twenty-five countries which will be involved in this area of the so-called developed world. Among the developing countries there is considerable interest in this field, and there may be another ten to fifteen who are on the road to such legislation, a bit differently constructed, but nevertheless protecting certain interests of individuals, companies, governments and national activities.

What is the common denominator of this type of legislation? Let us particularly refer to the European model. It has five basic characteristics:

1. The laws of general application are omnibus laws, comprehensive laws.

2. They establish basically an independent authority very close to the suggestion for a Data Protection Authority.

3. They establish rules for fair information practices, some more elaborate than the Data Protection Committee, but very few differing substantially from that set of seven principles.

4. They call for registration, licensing or otherwise reporting the existence and character of such personal record systems.

5. They establish legal penalties or enforcement machinery to see that these laws and any abuses to our personal data are dealt with.

Because of this trend, a number of years ago several international organisations felt that they should be concerned with the developments, partly generated by the technology, the introduction of computers, but also because this seemed to be an area which, in the human rights context, needed a bit more fulfilment than the very general statements you find in the United Nations Declaration of Human Rights or the European Human Rights Convention.

So we have five organisations which we could identify. The United Nations has taken this up in Unesco in the Commission on Human Rights, but there is unlikely, on a world level, to be anything forthcoming in the next few years. The Nordic Council discussed this and, I think in true Nordic fashion, they considered three years ago whether they should have a Nordic agreement, convention or other instrument. They rather rightly sat down and said, 'Well, the reason you need a convention or a legal agreement is when you cannot agree on something. And we Nordic people think we can agree', and therefore they abandoned the idea and they will have five laws of a complementary nature in those countries. They will not have an agreement; they will try to co-operate without that device.

The European Economic Community has been working on the issue, particularly in the context of data processing activities, and, on the other side, since 1974 the European Parliament has been concerned, and there is a possibility under one article or another of the Treaty of Rome that there would be a directive to the nine member states of the European Community.

Then there is the Council of Europe, which Roy Harrington will discuss, and finally, the OECD.

I should like to make one observation about this whole scene if I may. I think there is some confusion as to where Britain stands in it — ahead, behind, or differing or following the same track. I think in a sense there are two stages of data protection. There is the first stage, where a country decides the role of the government or public law that defines the interest to be protected, tries to find out the wrongs which might be engendered by misuse of information. That is stage one. These are the three principles which are more prominent in the Data Protection Committee Report — the establishment of an authority, the identification of interests and rights, and penalties.

The second stage is basically how to fit or tailor or balance the interests of particular applications, of particular problems. This is the code of practice.

The Europeans have all adopted and tend to adopt stage one. That is the principal and most important stage in a rather growing and changing environment in data protection. The UK, either because of its constitutional traditional background or the lateness of the hour, is dealing with stages one and two at the same time. Therefore, there is some confusion as to the codes of practice and all the details. It is in a way putting the cart ahead of the horse, because you must have a law before you have the codes of practice, and those may evolve over some years. This is clearly what is happening in Sweden, France, Germany and the other countries. They have a law of general rules. They are making codes of practice, but they do not call them that because that is not in their legal tradition.

The United States is in the same situation. It looked over the field after it passed its Federal Act and said, 'We are going to have codes of practice, but we are going to call them sectoral laws' and President Carter will soon announce a bundle of half a dozen to a dozen sectoral laws — codes of practice — the same thing. But they are basically the second stage.

As to the OECD, which is my principal mission, an essential difference exists between the OECD and the Council of Europe. As you know the history of the Council of Europe, it is particularly concerned with legal co-operation, human rights and that area. The OECD, which emerged following the termination of the Marshall Plan in 1960, is committed to more commercial and economic issues; it is concerned with energy, it is concerned with co-operation of a scientific and technical nature among the fourteen Western countries. And its mandate is to try to see that those countries to the largest extent possible, through co-operation and through mutual reinforcement of various activities, progress along the same lines and are harmonising themselves.

Therefore, OECD does not draft a great many conventions and treaties. They do some. They have everything from a road agreement on road safety to the atomic energy agreement, and now the question of petroleum. But basically they are working with central governments to reach informal understandings, to educate and cross-pollenise themselves so that they do not need to have conventions or treaties. Therefore, in this field of data protection the OECD countries feel that they can, at the outset at least, live with what are called guidelines — non-binding agreements, morally accepted by the member states, to be carried out in the first instance by the country in the form that their constitution and traditions suggest; and secondly, that a co-operation mechanism, an updating, an exchange of ideas, would exist permanently through the OECD, because it has a committee system, and your Government is represented on all phases of the OECD work.

So in this field the OECD actually began as a spin-off of the old work of the computer utilisation group. The concern in the late sixties was applications, manpower, standards, the growing integration to telecommunications, the trade dimensions. Out of that came the social dimension — not particularly the human rights dimension, but basic data protection. Data protection is an administrative reform of present practices, an administrative structure imposed on record-keeping practices. So within the OECD, because it is a servant of central governments, the governments have been interested in how they should adjust to this new administrative set of conditions on record-keeping practices.

Basicallly, that is where it started in the early 1970s. Most of the people were concerned with data processing. The data processors were developing their applications in a certain way, and now, because of the impact of data protection, they would have to consider different ways of doing things.

The OECD got more involved in 1977, due to a conference in Vienna which many of you will have heard of, because the question of trans-frontier, transborder, transnational data flows was raised. OECD is particularly concerned about the internationalisation of the issue, rather than the domestic activities. The OECD decided that they should have a working group particularly devoted to the question of guidelines, which could be agreed upon by the OECD countries and would in a way put an umbrella over this area. Many people feel that it is rather a sham to say that some countries which have no law are completely unprotected, and other countries, which have a law, are *ipso facto* completely secure in the protection of personal data. Neither is the case, but many countries are agreed that they wish to do this in their own way — including, by the way, countries such as Japan, who feel that this is a total new experience for them. The Japanese recognise that their data bases are connected very much world-wide and they have to get on the same bandwaggon.

The Australians look at it in a different way. They feel that they could easily get cut off. They are totally dependent in certain ways on this open flow of information. So in the context of free competition, trading of information, goods and services, the OECD is premised on a course which says that this data protection should not constitute a barrier to traditional open practices. This is to some extent a bit different perhaps from the Council of Europe, which has suggested that data about individuals should pass country borders only when it is protected in a certain way. In other words, there was a negative sort of connotation originally in some of the discussions within the Council of Europe, whereas the OECD feels that data protection should not affect the normal flow of commerce, of goods and services and of individual information where it takes place.

OECD's working committee met for the second time in December 1978. They are working on three draft documents and trying to integrate them. Basically, the difficulties lie in the Anglo-Saxon approach to this sort of problem which is a curative approach, and the European view which is a rather proscriptive approach. Particularly countries such as Australia and the United States find it very difficult to accept the European view on this sort of issue, and they are coming together very slowly. But the Council of Europe draft is one piece of the puzzle. The OECD has proposed a compromise draft, as it were, and in the centre there is the United States proposal following basically the fair information practices which have been the cornerstone of their privacy activities.

They are attempting to integrate these approaches. We have a very able chairman — a judge from Australia, Justice Kirby — and he is trying to meet the deadline which is July 30th 1979, so that OECD can agree informally with the member states, submit the document through the Council, which is the ambassadors at OECD, so that there will be an umbrella, non-binding as it is non-enforceable, but nevertheless a concurrence accommodated between the countries of OECD. Then, within it perhaps, we will have the Council of Europe module for Western European countries, a Nordic concern, an EEC concern, a Mediterranean concern — and so on. And over all that, there will at least be some general frame of reference.

7.2   The Contribution of the Council of Europe

Roy Harrington, Home Office,
Chairman of the Committee considering
the draft Council of Europe Convention
on Automated Data Files.

I should like to link in with what Russell Pipe has said, to explain what the Council of Europe is doing and what my role in it is. He explained the different membership of these different organisations, and it probably causes some horror that these different international organisations are all thrashing around in the same field. It is a little confusing, but in fact their roles are slightly different, partly in relation to their different membership which Russell Pipe has mentioned, and partly — which I should like to emphasise — in the nature of the end result. There is, as it were, a hierarchy. The OECD, which has geographically the widest membership extending in particular to the United States, Japan and Australia, is in this context working on producing guidelines, the purpose of which Russell Pipe explained. Next up the hierarchy in the 'sharpness of teeth' is the Council of Europe, the end result of which would be perhaps a Convention — in a sense, a form of international treaty — the application of which, however, in any particular state would depend entirely on whether or not that particular state chose to subscribe to it. So their result would be optional, but if they were opted for, legally binding principles. Finally, with the sharpest teeth of all, there is the Brussels machinery, the Common Market machinery, the end result of which is or could be a directive which, by virtue of the European Communities Act, once agreed would have the force of law in this country.

Turning my attention narrowly to the Council of Europe, which is what I am here for, can I explain my position in this. I am afraid, indeed, that the groups which work on this subject are indeed called groups of experts, but that, so far as I am concerned, is where the expertise stops. It is also the case that people who attend such meetings attend not as representatives of their government, but in a personal capacity, the purpose of which is to free the discussion a bit so that governments do not regard themselves as bound in any way by the end result which eventually appears. So, when I attend in Strasbourg, I attend to some extent in a purely personal capacity, and may I perhaps emphasise that that goes most strongly for anything I say here. I am not in any way speaking as a representative of the Home Office or the Government. I am attempting purely to describe what has been going on in the Council of Europe.

The problem is a relatively simple one and it is common to all these three areas, that different countries — particularly in Europe — are establishing legislation, differing subtly or perhaps quite extensively from one country to another, to protect the privacy of principally their own citizens. And if their regulations or laws are not very easily to be circumvented by simply taking the data across the border and doing the work somewhere else, some of them are instituting controls to limit or otherwise police the way in which data may be sent abroad.

There is an obvious danger that incompatible regulations in different countries will, in one way or another, clog up the works of international communication where it relates to personal data, either simply by making it a little bit more difficult or more expensive, or by actually stopping it. The Data Protection Committee's report refers to instances where, for example, British firms have been unable to accept business from Sweden.

The attitude — at, I emphasise, the personal level of those of us taking part in the Council of Europe discussions — is that we should not be setting out to establish a system of controls to police, in effect, cross-border traffic in personal data. I think that some of the drafts which have been circulated for wider consideration by the Council of Europe have, by misunderstanding on one part or the other, been interpreted, particularly, I think, on the other side of the Atlantic, as being in effect a way of erecting a regime of formalising internationally the barriers between the different regimes that are being established in European countries — a short step, indeed, to information protectionism.

That is obviously an acutely sensitive political point, and I do not want to comment on the merits of that. But I would simply say that that is certainly not our objective. If there has been a particular development since the earlier draft, it has been that the committee have been trying as best they can to put the current working documents into a form where they are intended to leave no doubt that the aim is to identify common factors — necessary common factors, minimum common factors — among the legislation of the different states, which — provided state A can be sure that those principles are being observed in state B, because state B is a signatory to the convention — will make it unnecessary to attempt to police passage of personal data across the border; in other words, to create an atmosphere or a regime of mutual assurance that common standards are being observed. Again, the principle is quite simple; the problem is that the practice gets extremely difficult when you are dealing with legislation which is significantly different. One then runs into the problem of trying to identify and reach agreement upon what are in fact the essential elements of different countries' legislation. One runs into the difference of legal practice, and, I think particularly relevant — I agree with much of what Russell Pipe was saying about trying to identify at what stage the UK is at the moment — one of the important differences is the extent to which, in some countries, certain matters are reserved for prescription by law, whether in the form of an Act of Parliament or subordinate legislation. That is one way of doing it. On the other hand, in some countries there is a much wider acceptance of different varieties of administrative discretion. This is one of the difficulties which I suspect international companies face in trying to find out what data protection means in a particular country, because in some countries the Act of Parliament is really quite a long way ahead of finding out what in fact the nuts and bolts of the system means, if you as a company operating in that legal system, want to process personal data.

The time scale of the Council of Europe's work is that we are to produce a draft convention by, I think, the end of July 1979. It remains to be seen whether we shall succeed in doing so to the extent of producing one which is agreed between the members of the committee. Let us assume optimistically that in fact we succeed. The result will then be made available to the committee of Ministers, after passing through various stages of what I might call the official hierarchy of the Council of Europe. I should like to emphasise that our work is work which in this country would be done by civil servants, only it is being done at the international level. The stage at which it moves into the political arena, where its political and practical acceptability is tested, is when it goes to the Committee of Ministers at the Council of Europe, and that stage is a little way off yet.

I have explained, I hope, what we are trying to do; perhaps I could explain how we are trying to do it. We are trying to identify common principles which would provide the sort of mutual assurance which I have described between participating states. And in doing so, it is relevant to the question of not setting up a sort of policing procedure for transborder data flows. We are trying, so far as possible, to operate by identifying principles in the hope that, to some extent, it may be possible not to go beyond prescribing what assurance should be provided, because the real difficulties start if you attempt to prescribe how that degree of assurance shall be provided. Different countries would want to achieve similar objectives in different ways, and the idea is that they should be left with that freedom.

I do not think there is anything very startling in the principles which we have identified. They are just another mixture of the principles which have been under debate on this subject for some years now. It might be relevant, perhaps, if I emphasised that the very considerable extent of overlap of interest between the Council of Europe work and the OECD work is very much recognised. They are not proceeding entirely independently, and indeed the next meetings of the OECD and the Council of Europe on this subject are being arranged in succeeding weeks so that we can try to get them into a reasonably compatible form.

Perhaps I should also explain the position, so far as we understand it, that the European Commission is in. The right of initiation of proposals in this area rests, in principle, with the Commission, though obviously a directive does not pass to the stage of being a directive unless it is acceptable at the political level in the Council of Ministers. The *raison d'être*, I suppose, of a directive instituted by the Commission would probably be in the context of freedom of competition, and the argument would run on the lines that, if different countries are applying data protection laws of different severity, there is perhaps an element of unequal competition between them. The European Commission has given some preliminary consideration to whether there is a case for seeing whether some harmonisation can be worked out for that reason and in that context. At the moment, however, they are conducting some preliminary research to try to establish what is the extent of the problem; what is the nature of transborder data flows within member countries of the European Community; what would be the costs and the practicalities of attempting some degree of harmonisation. That research, I suspect, is likely to take a year or so longer. I do not think it has an absolutely definite timetable.

So it looks as though the OECD and the Council of Europe horses are running fairly neck and neck, but they are not actually attempting particularly to compete with each other. The EEC, I think it is fair to say, is not yet at the stage of producing policy proposals because it is conducting some basic initial research.

Perhaps I could just add finally how difficult in practice this sort of queston does become at the international level, when you try to put together people, even though they are freed of bureaucrats' customary constraints of talking on behalf of their government or their department. It is very difficult to cope with the differences of different legal systems and different social attitudes. We have, in fact, an extremely varied membership, which includes Sweden, Holland, Norway for some of the meetings, but it is particularly relevant to say that the Common Law countries — the mainland European countries typically, our Common Market partners — and then, on the other hand, the Scandinavian countries, have really quite radically different attitudes to where to draw the line on what should be private and what should not and what should be the role of the state and what should not and what should be the role of an Act of Parliament and what should be the role of discretion of some sort of official. It makes it a fairly tall order to produce agreement, even at the level of officials. What will finally emerge after this sort of difficult problem has been considered at the political level I think I will refrain from speculating on.

7.3.   Developments in the USA

Trudy Hayden, former Director,
Privacy Project, American Civil Liberties Union

In the short time we have left I will just try to tell you some of the things that we have done in the United States which have turned out better than we had ever hoped, and some of the things that we have done which have turned out quite dismally and some things that ought to have been done that have not done — and leave it to you to decide what is applicable here.

We have several statutes on the Federal level and other statutes that have been passed by state legislatures which embody in statute form what will be your codes of practice. They proceed from the point of rights of individual privacy rather than data protection, and I think the strongest principle in all these statutes is the right of subject access. The major statutes, which I discussed in my paper are the Federal Privacy Act 1974; the Buckley Amendment, which applied to education records; and the Fair Credit Recording Act, which applies to credit records. We have a new one which has just been passed called the Right to Financial Privacy Act, which has not yet gone into effect — it starts in March 1979, I believe — which probably will not add much of anything. It is pretty much of a useless law I think.

On state level we have experimented with Medical Privacy Acts, with Employment Privacy Acts, a few timid experiments with rights of privacy concerning criminal justice records, which are not included in any of the Federal statutes.

The results of these statutes have been somewhat surprising. I think the most surprising result has been in the implementation of the right of subject access. Every one of these statutes proceeds with a right of individual access to records with some clearly drawn exceptions. Of course, there were great outcries when the Acts were passed and before the Acts were passed that these would be unworkable, and I think our greatest surprise is that they are workable, that the costs of implementing a right of subject access are surprisingly low. A conservative estimate of the cost of the first year of the Privacy Act turned out to be twice the actual cost, and the costs have gone down with each succeeding year. The administrative burdens have been negligible, with one very splendid exception — the FBI, which, I am sure you have heard, is a year behind in processing requests for subject access. There is a very good reason for that, which is that the FBI went absolutely crazy in collecting records about individuals and is now reaping its own rewards.

During the initial flurry, people get all excited about subject access, hysterical about it — there are always a few people who will spend their time writing away to every information system they can think of, saying 'I want to know what you have on me'. I think one of the reasons that the right of subject access under these statutes has worked out so well is that most of us have other things to do with our lives and our major reason for requesting access to our records is when we feel that there is a problem. Aside from the FBI records on political surveillance, the major reason that people have used the Privacy Act, which applies to the records of Federal agencies, are people who have been or are Federal employees, and they are interested in looking at their employment record. And I think that that is a perfectly understandable thing to do. People do not do this sort of thing because they are merely curious or because they are paranoid. They do it because a problem has turned up, because they are seeking other employment and they would like to know what their employment records contain.

The interesting second step is that all of these statutes provide for a right of correction, which is very, very seldom used. People fear that there are things in their record which turn out not to be there. Where corrections are necessary, most of them have been made very simply. If you read the report on the implementation of the Privacy Act, you will find that there is a fairly large number, although not the number we expected, of requests for access to records, but a very much smaller number of requests for correction of records, and only a handful of requests for corrections of records which were disputed by the agency which held the record.

So I think that the right of subject access, which was the most controversial point of all of these statutes, turned out to be not really a problem at all. Just having it seems to have created a sense of confidence in record systems which did not exist before.

The other thing which has proved very useful, although it has been something of an administrative burden and it is easy to make fun of it, is that every statute requires that record-keepers disclose in some way the purposes of their records and what is done with records; in particular, where records are going to be disseminated; what uses are made of records; and what other agencies or organisations will be given records. Under the Privacy Act 1974 this disclosure is implemented through publication in something called the Federal Register, which no person in his right mind would ever choose to look at. I do not know how many of you have seen the Federal Register. I am sure you have something similar over here. If you have insomnia it is good reading, but otherwise....

It is not the most effective kind of disclosure, but there is a way for people to find out what Federal record systems exist and what they are used for. And if you are willing to plough through all this bureaucratic language you can find out.

Those are the good things that have happened, and it really has made a change in atmosphere without an enormous administrative burden or enormous cost. There have been some snags. Where an agency or a record-keeper or a group of record-keepers have set out to circumvent the purpose of these statutes, it can be done. Let me take one clear example: the Buckley Amendment, which is a Federal statute which gives students a right to see their own education records, or parents of students under the age of 18. When the statute was passed the education community declared its intention of circumventing the law by not writing anything down. In fact, they did not write anything down for a while, particularly subjective impressions of students and references for students going from high school to university. That lasted for a while, but then it becomes very, very difficult and after a while you just fall back into the old ways. You begin keeping records again and you begin therefore implementing the Act, allowing students to see their own records. That change is beginning to happen. I think the academic community is beginning to relax its vigilance and its fear about committing student references to records.

The other thing that has happened in the Buckley Amendment is that students can be pressured into waiving their right to see records. Again, that was another way that the academic community attempted to circumvent the meaning of the implementation of the law. That is beginning to relax too.

So I would say that the things that were most feared when the laws were passed really have not come true, and in certain senses — in the procedural sense particularly — these laws are working very well.

But, there are some very serious problems to which I have absolutely no answer. One is the question of enforcement. There is no way that we have found for an individual to seek redress when some part of a privacy statute or a code of practice is violated. The device of seeking civil damages is really very clumsy in this kind of situation. If a piece of information was passed on to an employer, the information is clearly incorrect and that piece of information clearly cost the person the job, clearly caused a loss that can be measured in money, civil damages might be an answer. But that is not what really happens in most of these cases. There is not a tangible, measurable loss, and the device of civil damages has just not worked very well. Besides, bringing a civil suit is a very long and expensive and complicated procedure, and the stakes have to be quite high before you are willing to subject yourself to this kind of thing.

Administrative enforcement has also proved very clumsy. There have been attempts to set up tribunals and information boards. They always seem terribly remote, very slow to act, and no administrative mechanism has really been devised to deal with violations of the statutes. We have no oversight body; we have no licensing body which can go in and examine systems and examine the way they work and determine whether they are in fact following the dictates of the statutes. I do not know what the enforcement answer is for the United States, and I certainly do not have any suggestions for what it ought to be elsewhere.

Also, I think a very serious problem that we have is that the statutes deal very well with procedural rights such as subject access and rights of correction. They do not deal with purpose and collection of information and with uses of information, with the reasons that information systems are established and how they are used. We have no effective controls on the kind of information that can be collected and the purposes for which they can be used. There are a few meagre attempts tucked into various clauses of the statutes that exist. For example, the Privacy Act says that no Federal agency shall collect information which describes a person's exercise of free speech or freedom of religion — what we call our First Amendment rights — unless otherwise authorised by statute. As you know, the FBI and the CIA have for years been collecting information on how people exercise their rights of speech and association, and there has been no attempt to use the Privacy Act as a way of trying to limit political surveillance, and I do not think there is any chance that this could effectively be done. We have not looked squarely at information systems and asked: what are they for? What should they be for? What kinds of information systems ought to exist in the first place? That is completely unaddressed by any statute that I know of. It is also not addressed in discussions of public policy. I do not know what is happening here, but in America new information systems are being born every day. People think of new uses and interesting things you can do with information, and new information systems pop up.

Another thing that we have been unable to deal with is the device which we call record matching. I am sure there is a more technical phrase for it. What it means is that you take two existing systems and, without disseminating the information in any way, you just put them together; you match them up. And you see whether, for example, the same name appears in both systems, and that is supposed to tell you something. This began simply as an administrative device in the Department of Health, Education and Welfare as a way of catching people who were supposedly defrauding the welfare system. There is a whole system of welfare benefits, and supposedly there is a great deal of fraud which goes on in the welfare system. And a way of catching these people was to take, on the one hand, the Federal payroll, and on the other hand, the list in the

Department of Health, Education and Welfare of people who were receiving welfare. You put them on a computer and you match them together, and if you get my name on both you then investigate me and see:

1. Should I be receiving welfare at all if I am on the Federal payroll?
2. Am I receiving too much?
3. Am I receiving it by fraud or just by the stupidity or mistake of some administrator somewhere?

There is a great deal of argument about this in the States right now. President Carter is very enthusiastic for this kind of thing. The Federal Government is very enthusiastic for this kind of thing. There have been some embarrassing statistics that have come out of it as to whether we are in fact catching anybody and if we are not spending more money catching people than we are recovering when we do catch them. But that is not the point. The point is that we are taking record systems, matching them up together, and there are no statutes, no regulations, no principles which deal with this kind of record matching. We are simply circumventing all the very careful protections that we set up when we passed the Privacy Act and all the other statutes. Nobody has ben able to deal with this sort of thing. If you think about it, what we are doing with record matching is making it unnecessary to have that one big central computer — that big dossier — which contains information on each person from cradle to grave. It is not necessary to have one central data bank when you can simply take existing systems and match them up at will.

Since HEW began this programme, everybody has become infatuated with this idea and the number of proposals for record matching systems would make your head whirl. As I say, there is not only no law dealing with this, but not even any sound body of principle. Even those of us who have been dealing with privacy legislation for years have not the foggiest notion what to do about this.

It is having also the effect of increasing the use of the universal standard identifier, which in the United States is your Social Security number. If you have a common identifier for separate systems, it makes it easier to match up the systems. And record matching has given tremendous impetus to the spread of the use of the Social Security number as the common identifier.

Finally, something that was mentioned earlier is the advent of electronic fund transfer systems. When you read about them in the popular press it is known as the 'cashless society'. All transfers of money would take place electronically and you would never have to carry anything in your pocket. This is beginning in the States in very odd ways. We have certain regions where there is a proliferation of what are called point of sale services where you go to the supermarket and, instead of paying in cash, you put your little card in the supermarket register and money is immediately transferred electronically from your bank account to the supermarket's bank account.

We also have direct deposits of social security benefits — where the Government simply deposits directly into your bank account the money that you are due without sending you a cheque.

It is a very slow spread, because there are lots of practical and technical problems with this. But again, this kind of system really circumvents all the legislation that we have so carefully worked out. Nobody has stopped to think what is going to happen when the assistants are simply passing information around outside the borders of these discrete and separate information systems for which we legislated just a few years ago. There is a statute which just passed the Congress, which deals with electronic fund transfers. It does not deal with the privacy problems because no-one can figure out what they are.

I know that we are very close to the end of the session, so I am just dropping these things and leaving them. We have absolutely no answers to any of these questions. Our difficulty, in fact, in the States is even raising them in a way that anybody can understand. Those of us who consider ourselves experts do not understand them either.

With regard to the report which is under discussion at this conference, many of the things that you are considering will probably, when they are put into practice, work out a lot better than you think they will — if you follow our pattern. A lot of the fears have not come true. What will have to happen is that you will have to address — and we have to address — many of the things which really are not addressed at all by the report that we have been discussing.

7.4   Work of the Swedish Data Inspection Board
Rabbe Wrede,
Head of the Administrative Division, Data Inspection Board

The Swedish Data Act was the first piece of nationwide legislation designed to protect the personal privacy of the citizen. It came into partial force on July 1st 1973, affecting both the private and public sectors.

Concurrently with the Swedish Data Act the Data Inspection Board was established. Data Inspection Board is an agency of central government mandated to grant licences to the keepers of personal files and to monitor compliance with the Act. Anyone who wishes to set up a personal file must first obtain permission. Files that are set up by decision of the cabinet of Parliament are formally excluded from this requirement. Both branches of government must, as a practical matter, obtain a statement of opinion from the Data Inspection Board before taking any such decisions. Moreover, under the Data Ordinance, which is a set of regulations implementing the Data Act, these matters are to be dealt with in the same way as a licensing matter.

A person must be prepared to accept some infringement as a member of society, but the protection of privacy is therefore restricted to what may be regarded as 'undue'. In Sweden that has been a political question in the beginning, but not any longer I think. There are no political views on this matter for the moment. It is fully agreed by all the democratic parties in parliament who have the same opinion on these problems. So in working for the Data Inspection Board, we are not taking a political point of view. We have people with political backgrounds in our board and in the directorate, and that is enough for us. If there are any political problems and so on, we can always go to the directorate and perhaps write to the Cabinet and make them solve the problem.

Further, the licensing procedure must take account of the feasibility of issuing directives for the file. Certain directives are mandatory. These have to do with the purpose of the file and which personal data are allowed to be entered in the file. But if considered necessary, directives may also be issued on how the data may be collected, the technical equipment that may be used, how the information may be processed, notifying registered persons of, say, analysis of information about them, which data may be retrieved from the file, to whom they may be released and how they may be used, how the data are to be preserved and sorted out, and finally, control and security routines.

If, when deciding to set up a personal file, the Parliament and the Cabinet do not at the same time announce directives for their use, it will be up to the Data Inspection Board to issue such directives. We just cannot say 'no' to the file. We have to say 'yes', and then we can give a lot of directives for this file, how they may keep it and how long they may keep it and so on.

Permission to set up certain types of personal files requires particularly compelling reasons if the responsible keeper is someone other than the government agency which under law or statute is mandated to keep such files. Examples of this latter are political registers and records of previous convictions. Special circumstances must be present for permission to set up a file which contains information about private persons as regards their illness, state of health, political or religious beliefs.

The licence may be granted with specified time limits. Should it nevertheless turn out that an approved personal file results in undue infringement of privacy, the Data Inspection Board may alter given directives, issue new ones or remove the licence.

If there is reason to suspect that any item of personal information is incorrect, the responsible keeper is under an obligation to verify it. Should it turn out that the suspicion was well grounded, the item shall be rectified or excluded.

Under a separately issued directive a responsible keeper may be obliged to notify, either for the moment or on a sustained basis, a registered person as to the content of a personal file. However, the Data Act includes the general rule which gives a registered person the right to receive notification once a year at his request. In principle, this notification ought to be furnished free of charge. This was one of the big issues for the private sector when the Data Act was implemented in 1973. One of the big firms in Sweden was very upset about this, and I went back to them four years later and asked, 'How many people have come to you and want to see your file?' Just one person in four years! So there was no problem at all with it.

Some government agencies have had some problems. The National Bureau of Statistics had around 20—30,000 people asking in just the first six months to look into the files at what was registered about them. And the National Bureau of Statistics has about 160 different files about people.

The Data Inspection Board is not only a licensing agency. It also performs monitoring functions and is called upon to act as a wailing wall for the general public. For this reason the Board is entitled to inspect computer centres and other premises where automated data processing (ADP) is being done or where the equipment for ADP or input media is stored. This inspection right holds for all installations and not only those where information about persons is regularly processed. But as a matter of course the inspection right is limited to making sure that ADP does not lead to undue infringement of personal privacy.

The responsible keepers are obliged to furnish the Data Inspection Board with information needed for control purposes: for instance, about systems documentation and computer programmes. Moreover, the Board is entitled to make arrangements for computer runs and if the responsible keeper does not have the hardware at his own disposal but resorts to someone else — for example, a service bureau — the obligations to assist the Board for control purposes will rest on that service bureau. When we inspect a computer installation we usually — in 90—95% of all cases — telephone them and ask if it is OK to visit on such-and-such a date, and make an appointment and then we go there to meet them. In a very few cases we just call them in the morning at 9 o'clock, and we do that only when we suspect that illegal processing is going on. I have done it four or five times, and in every case there was something illegal. The last case went to court and the head of that firm was sentenced to pay just a small amount to the state because he had done something wrong. He had a customer file without a licence from the Data Inspection Board. But mostly, we do it very softly — we call them and make an appointment, and I think that is necessary. If we are too hard we do not get anything at all out of it.

If the Data Inspection Board is refused admission to premises or access to documents, the responsible keeper may be ordered to pay a fine. Obviously, the inspection activity must be carried on in such a way that it does not inflict unnecessary costs or inconvenience on the responsible keepers.

Responsible keepers who feel that decisions by the Data Inspection Board have gone against them may lodge appeals. A similar right of appeal is vested in the Attorney General who watches over the public interest. Complaints are handled by the Government in the Ministry of Justice.

In addition to administering the Data Act, the Board acts as licensing and supervisory agency with respect to two other laws — the Credit Reporting Act and the Debt Collecting Act. Both these laws regulate files irrespective of whether they are kept manually or with the aid of ADP.

So far the Data Inspection Board has received around 24,000 applications pertaining to about 30,000 personal files. On average, the name of every adult Swede appears on at least 100 personal files. With a population of roughly 8 million, Sweden is one of the most computerised countries in the world. The number of applications and the stringent rules of the Data Act really evoke a mental image of a vast bureaucracy, but in the space of about five years the comparatively small work force has managed to promulgate around 22,000 decisions — a figure that takes in a great many more personal files and at the same time discharges the board's basic supervisory duties.

The Data Inspection Board has deliberately sought to avoid bureaucracy. Around 65% of the agenda items are routine matters. For them the Board has developed, on the strength of the Data Act and within the framework of this law, a standard operating procedure — SOP — and that is 65% of all applications and perhaps 90% or 95% of all from the private sector.

No more than 40 or so decisions have been appealed against — and that should be seen in the light of approximately 22,000 decisions taken so far.

Occasional exceptions apart, it may be contended that the Data Act has entailed no more than marginal direct costs for the responsible keepers. The Data Act has some positive effects to its credit. Sometimes it has directly contributed to the avoidance of duplicated effort. Further, the board's activities have given society insight into computerisation and its consequences in several respects alongside the privacy issue. Among many areas to which attention has been drawn as side effects, mention may be made of the problems bound up with the security and integrity of data, the flow of data across national frontiers, the need for data quality, and so on.

Questions and Discussion

Question:

I was not clear whether the Inspection Board can be as flexible with the directives as it is proposed that the Data Protection Authority shall be with the Codes of Practice.

Mr. Wrede:

I think they are quite flexible. We can deal with a lot of problems and not only with the files. We can go a little step further and talk about how you may use output information and the hard copies from the computer — we can give directives about that too, and how long you may store these hard copies.

Question:

On the same point, am I not correct in believing that the directives are specific to a particular installation and are linked to a particular licence?

Mr. Wrede: Yes.

Questioner:

And in that sense, the system is more flexible than a Code of Practice in that it can be tailored specifically to the requirements of one installation.

Mr. Wrede:

Yes, and if we have a large number of similar files, we give them the same directives. But we deal with one at a time.

Hugh Pitcher, National Computing Centre:

It is proposed in the British legislation that there should be of the order of 50 Codes of Practice to cover the whole field. Would I be right in supposing that you have thousands of lists of directives tailored to each individual installation?

Mr. Wrede:

Yes, we have 22,000 licences, and every one contains at least two directives — mostly more.

Chairman — Edward Cluff:

In the DPC report it is proposed that there shall be a Code of Practice for a class of application, for instance, payroll. So everybody who is running a payroll shall confirm to that Code of Practice. So far there have been 37 illustrated applications, and some people think there might be a total of 50 or a few more. If we have 50 classes of applications and you appear to have a number of thousands of directives, is it fair to compare one with the other?

Mr. Wrede:

My personal point of view is that these 50 will not be enough. You cannot fix it with that. It is not enough, because every installation or every file is so different from the others. You have a different purpose, and so on. But in the payroll system or customer files or member file or something like that it is OK. This is standard operating procedure that I was talking about, which covers at least 90% of the private sector. But when you come to the Government files, the Government systems, it is not enough. Every one is different from the other. I think it would be very difficult to do it that way.

Alan Benjamin,
Director General, Computer Services Association:

If you have 100,000 directives, and a large number of them are very similar and grouped together, they become Codes for practical purposes. I think the essential difference is public sector files, where each class of use is very specific, or potentially so. They are very different from, if you like 90% of the applications in data processing in the private sector where, to all intents and purposes, you can classify them under a Code. Flexible enough, I would have thought.

Mr. Wrede:

The system in Sweden does allow that degree of flexibility down to installation level even in the private sector, although I accept that the vast majority of installations would fall within what you might regard as a Code of Practice.

Russell Pipe:

I would make the observation, though, that some people, particularly outsiders trying to study the Swedish experience — there is a little reservation that this tends to be quite *ad hoc*. People have found it difficult to trace patterns as you would in a Code of Practice. You would group together certain activities and you would have a guideline as to the parameters, let's say, where you might be able to move, but in the Swedish case-by-case approach, even though the directives are open, it does incur a lot of difficulty for organisations, particularly outside Sweden, to figure out exactly how they might apply. But some organisations feel that, even if they are not doing business in Sweden, they would like to know for company strategy what is going on, and I feel that the suggestion of *ad hoc,* case-by-case example for the Anglo-Saxons makes them feel a little bit uncertain where they are going.

Mr. Wrede:

Yes, but let me point out that some companies in Sweden feel uncertain too. In that case, let us say they want to start a new system. We do not want to put in Sw.Kr.100,000 into this and then go to the Data Inspection Board and the Board says no. That is not business. So they go to us at the beginning and ask how we treat similar cases, and we help them out and give them alternative solutions and try to be as open as possible and try to give them several new solutions to their problems. That is the way to deal with it. The DPC report says that the Data Protection Authority should be open and so on, and I think that is a very good point. Otherwise, you have got problems of bureaucracy and so on. You have to be open, you have to be open to discussions and so on at an early stage when you are developing a new system, and long before you implement it.

B. Buckroyd (ICL):

If I were in Sweden and you were inspecting me, I would like to say to you that I have a sales ledger system which is intended to identify other companies but may accidentally identify a person who is a customer. I wish to tell you nothing further about it except that I will agree that I will not disclose anything on that file to a third party. I also have an employee record system. I shall be quite happy to give you the file layout, the details of what is on that and what it is used for and again declare something in the order of what we will use that data for and what we will not. Would you accept that from me? What would you accept?

Mr. Wrede:

You must give us all the information that we want. On both systems, yes. Because accidentally you may have a private person in that customer file. In that case you have to have an application, a licence for it. Even if it is, not one or two, but five to ten. Let us put it this way. We even go to manufacturers and get the list of all their customers so I can go out and find all the computers in Sweden. And they give it to us, and we say we will keep it and when we have looked at it we send it back or we destroy it or we lock it up. And so we will do with your customer file too. And no-one working for the Data Inspection Board is allowed to tell any third party about this. In that case he will be taken to court and punished. So you have to give us all the information we want. At the start in 1972-73, when I was working for the service bureau we were quite upset about this, but it is no problem really because we do not want papers or information that we do not need for our supervision. We select the information.

Question:

Can I ask what check there is that you as an organisation do not abuse your own power? Who is your watchdog?

Mr. Wrede:

Who guards me? Let's put it this way. If I misuse my power, someone will know that sooner or later. In that case you can go to the District Attorney and tell him and he will take me to court immediately. And I will probably not be working for the Government any more. Unemployed from that day.

Paul B. Whitehouse, Northumbria Police:

You said in answer to the question from the gentleman from ICI that you require a user to tell you everything. You said earlier in your speech that in general you go along with prior notice to users, but occasionally you turn up unannounced to conduct spot checks because you suspect things. If a user has declared to you that he has five files, how do you expect to be able to discover that he has a sixth file without spending weeks and weeks and weeks at his installation?

Mr. Wrede:

That is a question we always get, and I say no-one has a file just for fun. You use it in some way, and sooner or later some private person writes to us, calls us, or something like that and asks us, 'Do they have a licence? Why does he use it like that?' and that is how we discover this file I talked about which was sent to court. They only had it for two months, and then a private person called us and asked just a simple question about it and we looked it up.

Question:

You have no knowledge, of course, about the users who have not created a worry to a citizen who has written to you.

Alan Benjamin:

I want to return to the comparison of the directive to a particular installation and the Codes of Practice, because I think it is an important point. One of the things which it seems to me that the Data Protection Committee's report offers is a positive side that you can actually approach them and address them and say, 'We have a file' or 'We intend to design a file. Does this suit you from the point of view of the Act?' If you did that you might find a queue at that door. You would also have to have certain skills in the DPA which I expect they do not want. So it does occur to me that if you have Codes, you are given a framework in which to work. You do not have to apply beforehand. And I suspect that the Codes will have in them some kind of instructions relating to the sensitivity of the data which are being used. I think that is one of the strengths of the report, that it addresses the use of data and not the file.

Question:

Auditors, whether internal or external, may get a hint of something and wish to make some interrogation of a file, create their own file, message date in order to discover whether there is accidental or deliberate misuse of those files. What sort of protection does one have under the Swedish system?

Mr. Wrede:

It is difficult to get a straight answer on that. I do not know if I can give you a good answer to that question. I will think about it and come back to it.

Russell Pipe:

I should like to raise a question which I think is a live one because of the Swedish experience. In their Act, unlike what will probably come out in Britain, Section 11 of the Act says that the Data Inspection Board — this is the kind of provision that is in several other laws — must take special note when an application comes along that the data should be processed, stored or used abroad, and that the Data Inspection Board should give permission for that transfer or use abroad when it can reasonably expect that similar protections will be afforded to the data. I wondered if our speaker could comment on the experience of Section 11 and how the Board views the transport of data to countries such as Britain which do not have reciprocal or equivalent laws.

Mr. Wrede:

When I first came to the Data Inspection Board at the first directors' meeting, I was quite shocked by the way they were looking at this problem. There was a hospital in Sweden which wanted to do small plastic cards from a magnetic tape, and this machine was not in Sweden at that time, so they had to take the magnetic tape abroad — to London, I think — and this machine was punching out those plastic cards. And the Board said no to that, and I think it was ridiculous — my personal point of view. Nowadays, let's put it this way. If you just store the data abroad and are not giving away any data abroad, just processing it abroad, you get 'yes' to your application and you get a licence. But if you send information abroad — process and send it away — you will probably get 'no' so far. But there is a Data Inspection Board in West Germany now, and there will be one in Austria and one in Denmark — there is one Denmark from 1st January 1979 — and there will be one in Norway, and so on. Then it will be very easy because we can tell them to go in an inspect, and there will be no problems at all to get a licence for such things. This is a problem in Scandinavia because two or three of the big service bureaux have one branch in Stockholm, one in Copenhagen and one in Oslo, and they will want to send information by wire to the computer which has the most overflow time at the moment and process it there. If you follow Section 11 you have to have a special licence for that and I do not know if they have one. I think they do it anyway.

Question:

Can I expand on that point and ask not just about Sweden. Has anybody experience of how many countries are refusing to send information? How much business are we losing by not having data protection yet? Does anyone know?

Alan Benjamin:

The identification of the flows of personal data across borders is very difficult. We suspect it is quite small. It is probably largely limited to multinational information about their personnel. That is not all it is, but it may be limited to that. We just do not know what the extent of personal data flow is. If you go beyond that and talk about data flow on legal questions or companies, it is very extensive. And if you interfere with that mechanism you go down a dangerous track. But the answer is that we do not know. It touches on the earlier point of audit. It seemed to us that these were practical matters of security and there are four kinds of security. There is contractual security; there is organisation security; there is physical security; and there is technical security. And in each of these areas organisations can do something about the data, particularly if it is sensitive. One of those areas is agreeing with auditors at the outset that they shall have certain contractual rights, and organisationally arranging for those auditors to access the files. These are practical matters. They are not particularly related to data flow.

Professor Paul Samet:

One class of personal information that is obviously distributed from one country to another is the stuff that goes to Interpol. But the other thing I wanted to ask: if your Data Inspection Board wants to send stuff to Norway, Denmark, Austria, who gives you a licence to do that?

Mr. Wrede:

The Ministry of Justice. We do need a licence. We are a modern agency, so we have our own information system about all the licences we have given. It is stored on the database and we have a terminal system.

Keith Williams, IBM Europe:

Can I add some information to this question of how much information is being lost on transborder data flow regulations? You have got to remember that only Sweden and Germany have a law which is currently in operation — only those two countries. There are three well-publicised cases in Sweden, one of which has been referred to, where data was not allowed to go abroad. But you have got to remember at the same time that, for example, banking transactions, airline reservations systems, are all operating quite normally. There is no impact on systems like that which have information about individuals. Very recently the Swedish Data Inspection Board has given permission to Unilever and to Rank Xerox to operate quite extensive personnel data systems that collect data from around Europe and operate outside Sweden. So the impact in Sweden is not very great. In Germany you have a different system. You do not have to go to a Data Inspection Board. You simply have to meet certain conditions which are set out in the law, and as long as the data is being sent abroad for a legitimate business purpose — i.e. to meet a contractual relationship or a quasi contractual relationship — and you are satisfied that the interests of the person concerned are not injured thereby, there is no restriction. I am not aware of any system which has changed its method of operation since the German law came into effect through that particular consideration.

Questioner:

Is Britain losing out because we do not have any laws? Are we restricted from getting data into this country from other countries who have laws because we do not have laws as strict as, say, Sweden?

Alan Benjamin:

There is no evidence that any of the laws impact on the flows of data, as Mr. Williams says.

Question:

In Sweden we have heard of your interest in files. May I ask whether that interest extends to the matching of information in files which may be separately and severally registered perfectly appropriately but which, within modern technology, can be co-ordinated for information purposes across quite wide distances?

Mr. Wrede:

If we have two different systems with different licences and they want to do some matching, they have to have a new licence for that matching. If you look at how it is done in the computer, technically it becomes a new file for just the moment when you write it out. And you need a licence for that.

Questioner:

This would not extend to ephemeral matching, transitory matching, momentary matching of files for a specific purpose at a point in time with no record other than the knowledge that has been gained?

Mr. Wrede:

Every file must have a defined purpose, and if you go outside that purpose you have to have a new licence. To deal with it for a new purpose you have to have a new licence — alter your old licence for this new purpose.

Chairman:

I should like to comment on that myself. This is precisely why some of us like the concept of controlling the application and we say that the file itself is an inert, harmless thing until you have done something with it. Therefore you control what you do with it. A particular file in one application can be quite harmless. The same file on another application can be quite damaging. Therefore, we believe, control the application now. Trudy Hayden referred to the problem in the United States. They have not yet come up with the answer. You have two files and you match the records together. The output of those matched files can be quite damaging, and what we submitted was that you have then created a new application, and it is the application you have controlled. So if you have one application and another application with two separate files, you put them together, you make a third application, you must have a licence or be registered for the new application. That to us seems to be a completely effective control.

Questioner:

In Sweden how do you decide which files must be licensed and which ones do not have to be?

Mr. Wrede:

Every file that contains a personal, private individual.

Chairman:

All files that contain personal names and addresses must be licensed.

Questioner:	Even on a home computer?
Mr. Wrede:	Yes.
Questioner:	So someone's Christmas Card list?
Mr. Wrede:	Yes. That is our big problem now!

Questioner:

Could I take a particular example of this question of slightly changed use. The Registrar General in England, Wales and Scotland by statute gives health authorities computer tapes of births and deaths. The normal use I make of the tapes I get is looking at birth rates or looking at particular death rates. But let us say that tomorrow I am using, say, a statistical package of many ones that are readily available and I decide to look at the data in a different direction. Would I need a different licence for that? In other words, normally I am looking at, say, just the birth rates, but let's say I want to look at how long people have been married before their children were born. Would I need to get another licence to look at that? This is personal information because it has names and addresses.

Mr. Wrede:

If it is a new purpose, if you have not defined that purpose from the beginning you have to have a new licence. But if the purpose contains this new way of using your file, you do not have to have a new licence.

Chairman:

So you are saying that when you license the file you do define the purpose to which that file is going to be put, which to us is the application.

Question:

Are there any provisions in the Swedish Act for a data subject to be told in advance or be told at some time how the information he provided is going to be used or whether he can know who has used it?

Mr. Wrede:

We do that with specific files. We can give a directive to tell them. Before you do this you have to notify all the persons registered in this file as to what you are doing with it.

Questioner:

What kind of files would those be where you would do that?

Mr. Wrede:

Let us say, if you want to do a survey about what people like — if they like their fish and chips red or yellow or whatever! This kind of market survey. We often put it like this and say, you must tell them this information is stored in a computer and it is stored for two years or something like that, and it is not given away to any other third parties.

Questioner:

Do you insist on the same for medical files?

Mr. Wrede:

Medical files — yes. From the beginning this directive was set up in a conference with the Data Inspection Board and some university people and hospital people for medical files. And then we use it also in a little different way for these market surveys.

Question:

As an auditor, in this country we are empowered by the Companies Act to obtain information that is necessary for the purposes of our audit, and we use generalised software to extract information and manipulate information on our clients' files. I just wonder how we would be licensed in Sweden.

Mr. Wrede:

The audit control function is in the purpose of the customer file or book-keeping file or something like that. You do not need a new licence of that. It is already included. We write the purpose in that way so there is no trouble for the auditor at all.

Question:

What do you do for a new file to do some important piece of research. Do you find yourself in the position of having to say, 'Yes, this is an important piece of research. Therefore, you have a new file,' or 'No, this is not important and we will not allow you to have a new file'?

Mr. Wrede:

We may not tell the responsible people what they ought to do or ought not to do. It is not our business. If he wants to do something we just look upon it to see if there are any problems for privacy or not. If there is a problem for privacy for the person registered, we then perhaps give an alternative or something like that. We cannot discuss the background, why he wants to do that.

Questioner:

Suppose the application was of real national importance — for example, tracing the occurrence of an epidemiological outbreak through name and address? Would you find yourself in a rather difficult position?

Mr. Wrede:

Yes, but we can give some regulations round this file and tell him, do not do so-and-so; just keep to your purpose for this file. Then it is OK.

Question:

Returning to the question earlier about informing the subject to what purpose the data will be put, what protection does the data subject have when the owner of that file returns later and asks to use the file for an entirely different purpose than originally declared to the persons who gave the information?

Mr. Wrede:

If he is following the Data Act he comes to us first and applies for a new licence for this new purpose. And then we can tell him again, 'You have to go out to every individual'.

Questioner:

Does he have to go back to the people who are on that file?

Mr. Wrede:

Not regularly, but we can tell him to go back.

Question:

Could you say how many directives have been issued under Section 6(9) on security and control, and could you give us some examples of the directives that you issue on security and control?

Mr. Wrede:

I can give you one example, but I cannot tell you how many. One big firm, owned by the banks in Sweden — for credit reporting — had a large file of all Swedes over 16 years of age. They had their personal number, name, address, income and whether they owned any property, and so on — just to give credit information, credit reporting to the banks, and this was stored in one big database. When they first came to us we said to hem, 'Go back home. Look for any security problems and so on with regard to these points'. Then they came back six months later with a report, a thick one. And we said, 'Can you live within these rules and still fulfil your purpose?' and they said, 'Yes'. Then we settled down and we read it and pointed out a few things and so on. Then we had this set down, and they must follow this. If they want to change it in any way they have to come back to the Data Inspection Board for a new licence in that particular thing.

Questioner:

These are their own administrative procedures, rather than any technical security requirement?

Mr. Wrede:

They were looking at technical security too, and all kinds of security problems for that file.

Professor Samet:

You have said that there has been a fairly limited amount of abuse of the law. How much abuse do you think there would have been if the law did not exist? If you did not have your Act, you would be out of a job, but do you think the situation in Sweden would be any worse than it is at the moment? Has it all been worthwhile?

Mr. Wrede:

I must answer as a private person now. Yes! It is much worse because we are so computerised in Sweden, especially the public sector — not the private sector. If we did not have the Data Act I think there would be too many files about me as a private person stored, and they would spread out information to different agencies and so on without any control. And without my knowledge — I think that is the main point.

Question:

I was going to ask how the Swedes and perhaps we would deal with the question of things like muck-raking and gossip columnists. It is probably more a problem in the United States than Europe — where you gather information on public figures, specifically perhaps to embarrass them, but which is genuine material from their past, when they might have committed indiscretions, to embarrass them when they become prominent.

Mr. Wrede:

We have not had any application about that.

Questioner:

How could you control that sort of thing?

Mr. Wrede:

Control it? They must use it in some way. They do not have it just for fun.

Questioner:

But, because of the existence of computers, it is much easier to get this information. Could you stop people doing that?

Mr. Wrede:

Yes. We can stop them, because in Sweden we have the corresponding word to what is translated as 'soft data' — nothing to do with hard facts. Just gossip or thoughts about a person. There is quite a lot of discussion about this and nobody likes it — nobody in Parliament.

Questioner:

There is a class of files we have not really talked about — the question of electronically recorded data prior to printing for typesetting purposes. Things that come into this are trade directories of various sorts — there might be someone writing a biography or an autobiography, certainly in newspapers, and this could contain a lot of personal information. In Sweden do these come under the scope of Data Act, and if so, how do you control, because some of the information is quite transitory that is published?

Mr. Wrede:

You just use the file for printing purposes. Let us say, first, if you just use it for printing purposes you put it up from the magnetic tape to a printer. In that case it is outside the Data Act. It is not included in the Data Act. If you just use it for this purpose. But if you use it to retrieve information from it and make questions to that database —

Questioner:

At some stage I would, if I do an index to the book.

Mr. Wrede: That is also excluded.

Chairman:

Does this mean to say that you are controlling word processing systems then?

Mr. Wrede:

If you read the Data Act, it includes word processing. In practice we exclude it from the Data Act.

Questioner:

The media are specifically excluded from the data Act, are they not?

Mr. Wrede: No.

Questioner:

Is there not some provision with regard to the press having a special position?

Mr. Wrede:

No. Last week we found that one of the big morning papers had a file without a licence.

Question:

I should like to ask about patients' access to medical records. I understand that in Sweden patients do have access, subject to the right of a doctor to withhold that information if he thinks it will cause harm to the patient. But I also understand that the reserve power of the doctors is very, very rarely used. Could you comment on that, and perhaps Trudy Hayden could say what the situation is in the States as well?

Mr. Wrede:

The patients have the right to look at the notes made by the doctor, even if it is on paper. If it is stored in a database or magentic tape they also have the right to see them. But if it will harm him for the moment, one or two or three or four words can be excluded. Perhaps if the doctor has put down that he has cancer and the doctor does not want him to know that for the moment because it could harm him and he would get more sick for the moment, he can stop that kind of information. But if the person comes back a month later he has to look at it once more and say, 'No, we can't do anything about him' or 'Now we can tell him'.

Questioner:

Are you able to say to what extent doctors do withhold that information?

Mr. Wrede:

It is very difficult for the doctors to live with this rule. They do not know enough about it, so they do wrong sometimes — most times. That is my private point of view! I had a lot of people calling my office to tell me 'why can I not look up to see what is stored about me?' In nine cases out of ten the doctor had done wrong, because he has no knowledge about this set of rules. It is quite a wide set of rules and it is very difficult to read and it is difficult for a lawyer too. So it is not because the doctor has no education to read this. It is a problem.

Ron Lacey, Social Work Adviser, MIND:

I wonder if I could ask our Swedish colleague if there is any evidence that people have actually been harmed by this situation? This is the common argument, i.e. it is not in people's interests to see what is written about them; people are likely to have undue anxiety; all sorts of problems are likely to ensue. Lots of anxieties are expressed in that area, but in England yet we have not got the situation where we can actually measure what harm is likely to ensue except the professional opinions of the doctors who predict these sorts of consequences.

Mr. Wrede:

Let's put it the other way. What harm can it do if they know what is stored about them, what sort of information is stored about them?

7.5 Swedish Data Policy: An Overview

Kerstin Aner,
Under-Secretary of State, Ministry of Education, Sweden.

Background

Historically, Sweden belongs among the pioneers in computing. Industrial computer production was started as early as 1951 resulting in the successful all-Swedish electronic computer BESK (Binary Electronic Sequential Calculator) in 1953, a machine that at the time was considered to have the highest calculating speed in the world.

This advantageous situation, however, did not last long. Computer production has since then become more and more centralised, and smaller countries are having difficulties in keeping pace with larger efforts. This means that for the smaller country emphasis is increasingly put on the adequate use of computer technology, rather than on the production possibilities.

The computerisation of the Swedish society has thus quite rapidly concentrated on applications in private and public organisations and administrations. Especially since the middle of the 1960s, this development has shown a speed comparable with that of leading larger countries. Swiftly growing sectors are industrial data processing, public administration and office automation. This has been reflected by surveying efforts carried out by a number of governmental commissions that over the years have studied development possibilities in different fields of the Swedish society. Together, these reports constitute the background for the present Swedish data policy.

Most of these reports discuss data processing in the public sector. The major part of Swedish industry is in the private sector, and it is mainly carrying out its own rationalisation schemes. A minor part of Swedish industry is owned by the state. Industrially oriented data processing policies are therefore to a large extent taken care of by industry itself, without participation by public authorities. In the longer ADP-perspective though, certain co-operation is natural, for instance concerning data network communication, educational programs, research and development in the universities, and data processing legislation. The increasing employment problems in many sectors of society nowadays tend to increase the demand for deepened co-operation between the private and public sectors. This is natural not only in Sweden, and is reflected in the need for long term planning. This has influence on the structure of public ADP-systems.

Public information processing and data bases are exceptionally well developed in Sweden. There are large computerised systems for:
- population registration
- taxation
- judicial purposes
- social welfare
- employment opportunities
- vehicle and driver licence registration
- pollution registration
- land planning
- administration of personnel and salary files
- public accounting
- statistics
- and several other purposes

At present, measures are taken for centralisation of several of these systems, some of which at present rely on early and heavily concentrated system structures.

Below will be found a discussion of chiefly public investigations about needs for general policy measures in certain important areas of data processing concern. This reflects the expansion of ADP policy awareness in the Swedish society during the 1960s and the 1970s. Among the topics discussed, are privacy legislation, industrial computer production, data co-ordination, data networks, vulnerability in computing, effects on the labour market, and other areas of concern.

1. Privacy

In Sweden all citizens have for more than 200 years been granted free access to all unclassified public documents, e.g. documents that have been received or set up by central or local governmental agencies. This is considered as a fundamental principle in Swedish legislation. The principle was first touched by effects from computing after reports from a parliamentary commission in 1966. It was noted that the Freedom of the Press Act, a constitutional cornerstone in Swedish democracy, could in fact be affected by applying the new technology. This has been emphasised later on, in connection with privacy legislation.

The privacy problems were addressed by a special governmental commission in the early 1970s. After thorough, and in fact pioneering investigations, this commission proposed a bill to Parliament in 1972 suggesting a Data Act in order to protect privacy, as well as changes of some sections of the Freedom of the Press Act in order to maintain the citizen's right of access to the public information, even when such information was processed with the help of ADP. The proposal was accepted by Parliament in 1973 being the first of its kind in the world.

Concurrently with the Swedish Data Act the Data Inspection Board (DIB) was established. The Data Inspection Board is an agency of central government, mandated to grant licences to the keepers of personal files and to monitor compliance with the Act. It is headed by a director general, who is required to have experience of the bench. Its head office consists of three units: the licensing division, the supervisory division and the administrative secretariat.

Board activities follow the directions of an eleven-person directorate, with the director general serving as chairman. The other ten members are politicians from parliamentary parties, and persons representing the business community, trade unions and other interested organisations.

It should be pointed out that the DIB, like most other government agencies in Sweden, is an autonomous authority which administers the Data Act independently. Compared with its counterparts in many other countries, the typical government agency in Sweden has more the character of an administrative tribunal, with a large amount of independence towards other institutions.

According to a basic principle in the Data Act, anyone who wishes to set up a computerised file containing personal data must first obtain permission.

A licence shall be granted if there is no reason to assume that undue infringement of the registered person's privacy will arise. The kind of quantity of personal data entered in a file, as well as the attitude to the file of those who are to be registered are factors of importance in weighing the risk of undue privacy infringement that can be regarded as undue.

Special regulations concern the possibilities of filing personal data abroad. These regulations are meant to be adjusted to conform with later international agreements concerning transborder data flows.

In addition to administering the Data Act, the Board acts as licensing and supervisory agency with respect to two other laws, the Credit Reporting Act and the Debt Collecting Act. Both these laws regulate files irrespective of whether they are kept manually or with the aid of ADP.

The Data Act has means an important step forward. However, it has been a pioneer job, regulating a brand new technology. In 1976, therefore a new Data Act Committee (DALK), was appointed, with the objective to review the law in the light of the development and experiences so far.

The report of DALK, of August 1978, confirms much of the motives for the existing Data Act. This is to be kept as a basic form of legislation. However, adjustments are suggested on a number of points.

Suggestions are also given concerning further investigation of the problems around filing personal data with other means and methods than ADP. Here, a general Integrity Act can be expected in the long run.

2. Data Co-ordination

In 1972, the public Data Co-ordination Committee (DASK) was set up, with mainly the following tasks:

— to elucidate and codify the needs and opportunities for a co-ordination of administrative data processing between sectors and authorities, primarily within the national administration;

— to lay down guidelines for those areas where co-ordination should be focused;

— to consider the organisational forms whereby co-ordination is to be established and maintained.

The DASK Committee carried through fairly thorough background investigations, and has recently formulated proposals concerning:

— planning and co-ordination of public computing policies;

— decentralisation possibilities for certain structures;

— organisation of governmental data centres;

— system development methods and other topics.

These proposals will form a base for a governmental bill during autumn 1978.

3. Concern for Computer Industry

The increased concentration concerning the production of computer equipment that more and more has come to be regarded as inevitable, has motivated thorough studies about national policies in the field. Especially from Swedish viewpoints, remembering the early success with the BESK computer, the growing dependance of foreign production has raised questions about industrial integrity.

This field was first studied in 1972—74 by the Computer Industry Commission. Its work was divided between concern for how the use of computers was developing and concern for production of computer equipment itself. It was clearly seen that these two areas were closely related. The Commission noted that very strong efforts in research and development that primarily USA and Japan were implementing, and admitted that small countries had to be realistic about resource difficulties here. A certain production dependence had to be accepted.

However, the commission stressed that the use of computer systems needed strong support. Therefore it proposed increased efforts in education, basic research and development measures, data communication, and certain standardisation activities. It also added a discussion about public interest in the only Swedish large computer production company, Saab-Scania.

These proposals were later implemented, to some extent. The computer production problem, however, turned out to be difficult, and not until 1977 a strengthened semi-public company Datasaab was formed. Further, increased dependence on foreign suppliers also concerning electronic components has come more and more into focus. This problem is being specially reinvestigated in 1978. One can foresee limited possibilities for small countries also in this area. Research and development investment needs for micro-processor production are generally very high, which motivates a strong centralisation of efforts to those countries who have access to the resources needed. Some basic production, though, is to be furthered within Sweden, to keep up the component competence.

The National Industrial Board has recently published a report, drawn up by the Commission on the Computer Industry (SIND:1978:1), on the development of the Swedish computer industry and on the market trends for computers and data communication equipment. The report includes a forecast of the market trend for computers in Sweden, which points to an annual growth of more than 20%. Owing to an increased concentration on terminal based systems the market for terminals is expected to grow quickly. The proportion of small computers is also expected to increase.

4.   A Public Data Network

Many early studies reached the conclusion that a generally available public data network would support the development of Swedish computing substantially. Pressure was put on the Swedish Telecommunications Administration, Televerket, to increase the efforts towards this end. The development has been satisfactory, although harmonising with certain closely related countries has needed both time and expert resources.

A common Nordic public data network will be put in operation starting 1979, as a joint effort by Televerket and its Nordic counterparts.

The Swedish network uses circuit switching, with plans to offer packet switching possibilities in the beginning of the 1980s. It is a syncronous full duplex network, with transmission speeds of 600 to 9,600 bits per second. The higher speeds are to be added later. A number of services are being made available on the network. The planning stresses the need for security and reliability of the network, plus efforts at making the services generally available, throughout the country.

5.   Vulnerability

There has been no overall assessment of the risks involved in the entire field of computerisation. No such overall assessment has been made even within the civil service sector, even less for the country as a whole. Nor have any principles been put forward. The chief explanation would appear to be a lack of consciousness of vulnerability problems, a lack which for that matter is not unique to Sweden.

However, it is clear that data processing technology has greatly contributed to the increased vulnerability of the modern, highly industrialised society. It is also clear that this development is of great consequence to national security policy. Vulnerability can be critical not only — nor even primarily — in war situations, but also in situations when threats and pressures are directed against the country. The risks following terrorism activities also come into the picture. The vulnerability of computer systems can, therefore, be used against the community in all situations — ranging from deepest peace to war, by forces within and without the country. Therefore, these issues are of vital importance to the nation and thus also to the total defence.

These problems are being studied in detail by the SARK Commission, starting its work in 1976. The general conclusion is that vulnerability today is unacceptably high.

Many of the activities outlined by SARK, in the form of overall planning of the use of computers, are of such a kind that they should be the responsibility of Government, and met by decisions on special matters or by the promulgation of norms. There is, however, a prominent need for advice and information on certain questions. In SARK's opinion, therefore, it may be expedient to entrust tasks of a consultative character to some already existing body, and perhaps, too, such promulgation of norms as is not considered a government responsibility. The main task of such a body should be to advise on security questions.

6. Transborder Data Flow

Data processing technology cannot be isolated from other types of technology. It is a complement to other technology. For example, the need for, and the dependence on, well-functioning telecommunications technology and satellite traffic has increased. This dependence will increase in the near future as a Swedish public data network will be put into operation in 1979 to form part of a common Nordic network. Later on, this will probably be coupled to other national or international data networks.

There is an extensive flow of personal data across national borders. But we do not know how we depend on computers in other countries. The greater the flow of various kinds of data across national borders, the greater becomes the degree of dependence on stable political conditions both in the processing country and in those countries through which information is transmitted. Nor has dependence on international data banks in various areas of the community been satisfactorily analysed.

It is generally agreed in Sweden that something must be done before the transborder data flow causes extensive market dislocations, in light of lack of know-how on national levels, etc. There is a risk that the new dimension of transborder data flow will cause a national neo-protectionism, which can become troublesome. It seems to be a paradox, but nevertheless the free flow of information probably has to be regulated by international agreements in order to be kept free.

The transborder questions will be future tasks for expanded study.

7.   Computers and Labour

In the last decade computerisation has made its true breakthrough, and has affected working conditions in most branches of public administration, industry and commerce. It creates new opportunities for development that are important to use, but at the same time makes great demands on readjustment and renewal. The greatest changes probably still lie in the future.

Computing has so far been most extensive in the field of administrative data processing. The character of office work has already greatly changed. This trend is expanding. In the next few years increasing numbers of offices are expected to acquire electronic equipment for storage, processing, and output of printed data. Several of these systems are expected to use data network connections.

Computers are certainly also used for specialised tasks in the communications sector, e.g. for supervision and control of aviation, ships, telecommunications and railway operations. Extensive computer systems are used also in medicine for, e.g. patient data and clinical support.

In industry, computers are being increasingly used in various production processes. Automation is regarded in all industrial countries as an important means for increasing productivity. Here, industrial robots get more and more successful. About 600 industrial robots were present in Swedish industry in 1977. They are used, among other things, for heavy monotonous jobs and for jobs involving an unpleasant working environment.

It is probable that at many places computers have reduced the need for office staff. Unless the service sector continues to step up its total employment as rapidly as hitherto, computerisation in the office sector may lead to new and greater problems of unemployment. In other sectors, such as the graphic industry and parts of the communications field (post, telecommunications, shipping, railways, etc.) the introduction of electronics has meant that certain occupational groups now seem to be on the way to disappearing. This is also relevant for, e.g. the manufacturing industry.

With computerisation there also follows a number of new occupations. Many of them require specialised forms of education, which must often be revised to keep pace with new technical developments. Education in the data processing field is being given both at upper secondary school and on a number of post-secondary courses, as well as, and extensively, at universities. It is important that this education should in future be general enough to allow a choice between different jobs, while at the same time providing the special qualifications needed.

An interesting question is the extent to which a general relation exists between automation and job satisfaction.

The new technology may thus bring great changes both for better and worse. It places great demands on the ability for personal adaption. Adaptation may be difficult for the individual even when it offers the means for improvement of her/his situation.

Different questions of this kind have been brought up in reports both from the Confederation of Trade Unions and the Central Organisation of Salaried Employees, from political parties, and in discussion documents. On the international plane the International Labour Organisation (ILO) has issued a warning that too rapid a development may have serious consequences for employment.

The Swedish Parliament has in various contexts touched upon the need for investigation of the effects of computerisation and electronics on production and working conditions. A specialised commission has recently been appointed for this purpose.

It can be relevant also to draw attention to governmental efforts concerning new and electronic mass media. The informative, and financial, possibilities for text-TV and Viewdata are to be looked into thoroughly, starting autumn 1978. It is expected that such media will strongly influence the general public's information access in the future.

8. A New National Data Policy

Owing to the sweeping effects of computing a clearer policy must be framed and a better basis for future co-ordination of decisions concerning the use of computers and the acquisition of computer equipment.

Since the State, its departments and agencies and the local authorities, are among the most important groups using large administrative computerised systems, a policy must be found to govern this usage. The policy must include all effects which follow from the introduction of computers, both intended and unintended. No office or factory has yet been computerised without deep, sometimes, radical changes in its own nature. If the computer is to do its job properly, it puts demands on the accuracy and the regular flow of the work done outside it, demands that may be of an entirely new nature. In the initial stages (and these often continue for quite a long time), the computers demand more manpower than before, not less. It has also been shown in practice that large administrative computer systems seldom achieve lower user costs. They may, however, allow the administrators or workers to achieve better results, or different results, but the real cost-benefit balance is rather complex.

Because of these and other factors, guidelines are needed for a government data policy. They are needed for the civil service, and appear equally desirable for local governments and for industry and commerce. Action within the public sector automatically has repercussions also on the private sector. The long-term goals for the use of computing and its effects must be defined in order to create a better survey of such factors as usage areas, operational reliability, the influence of users and other staff groups on systems development and operation, other questions of employee participation, and efforts towards decentralisation.

Especially in view of the fact that the use of computing today is probably very much smaller than it is expected to be in future, a high-level Consultancy Group for Data Processing has been appointed to draw up the guidelines required for a deliberate data policy.

This group is chaired by the Minister of Budget, and consists of under-secretaries of state, members of parliament and experts.

A bill will be proposed to the Parliament during the autumn 1978 session.

Editor's Note:

Unfortunately, Kerstin Aner was prevented by weather conditions from attending the Conference. We include, however, the text of her speech which provides an analysis of current political debate about the workings of privacy legislation.

The Swedish Data Act of 1973 is already under review. This does not mean that the Swedes have already grown tired of it, but rather that they want to make it even more encompassing and secure. A Committee for overseeing the Data Act has been sitting since 1976, and has produced a paper last June. This paper has been sent round, in the Swedish way, to everybody concerned, in and out of Government, and is gathering a harvest of relevant criticisms and counter proposals. The Committee, in the meantime, is pondering another batch of questions, especially about public access to data.

The Data Act was and is specifically addressed to the *protection of privacy*. The Swedes still consider this danger their third greatest political worry (in an official opinion poll early in 1977). A vast majority of them dislike personalised advertising in their mail.

A small but interesting sample of people who refused to answer a questionnaire about their personal habits and opinions, sent out by the Central Bureau of Statistics in 1976, were interviewed in 1977 about why they did not wish to answer. An even smaller control group of willing answerers were also interviewed about their willingness.

One of the results of this probe was that *no-one,* whether they wanted to take part in the questionnaire or not, *really trusted the promises of anonymity.* To a greater or lesser degree, they all felt undressed, insecure, manipulated by the data-gathers.

As I said, this was a very small sample and can only be regarded as a pilot project. But there is reason to believe that it mirrors a prevalent opinion among Swedes, an opinion which in a way is irrational, would inflict on us even without them. But in another way the people are right, although for the wrong reason: because they do know very little indeed of the uses to which the data about them are put — especially the data which they have not provided consciously, but which are being lifted by the researchers from official files gathered for completely different purposes.

Behind and under this concern about privacy, two other questions are thronging in on the Swedish consciousness, in connection with computers. One is about *computers and labour,* and the other is about *computers and vulnerability.*

In offices and factories, computers are now being introduced at an accelerating rate. The trade unions in Sweden have worked a bit tardily to this fact, but are now working hard to make up for lost time. The debate in Parliament and the mass media slowly starts to attack this new subject. The Data Act Committee does not have the effects of computerisation on work environment on its agenda, but it will have to face one question at least: how much, and at what point in time and in what way, should the trade unions be able to influence personnel files and other uses of computers at work.

The vulnerability issue concerns Sweden very much, as one of the most technologically advanced countries in the world, especially as telecommunications are concerned, and also as a country extremely dependant on its foreign trade. The Defence Department is doing several studies of the vulnerability of Sweden to war and sabotage, and one of the most hair-raising of these is the one about computers. Not a bomb, but a few cheap, easy, well placed acts of sabotage, could immobilise the whole Swedish system of welfare payments and government salaries. There does not seem to be very much one can do about this by making laws, but it does play a part in stressing a general de-centralisation of the computer net, which will then have consequences for many other ways of using the computers of central and local government.

The most important part of the Swedish background to the Data Act I have not yet mentioned, because I think you are at least roughly familiar with it: the peculiar *openness* of the Swedish society. The presumption in Sweden is that any paper entering, leaving or stored in a Government office of any kind — including local government — is open to inspection by any citizen, without his asking permission or stating his reason. There are quite a lot of exceptions to this, but the legislator always has to keep this first assumption in his mind, even when dealing with computerised information.

The first point I will take up on the agenda of the Data Act Committee, concerns *whether permission must be given by* the Data Inspection Board to public or private bodies wishing to keep computerised personal files. The one reason for which such permission must be withheld, according to the law as it stands now, is that *personal privacy is endangered* by this file.

The question before the Committee was: do we confirm the practice of the Data Inspection Board so far, in granting or withholding permission or setting up conditions for it? In general, it was the consensus of the Committee that the DIB has done rather a good job and that we can be satisfied with it, and make the Act explicitly follow some of its practice.

One of these points is that no private organisation should be allowed to keep a file of *other individuals* than those it has a *real and close connection with*. A corporation may have a list of its customers, but not of prospective customers; a trade union a list of its members, but not of people they would like to have as members.

Another question is: what is to happen with those files that the *Cabinet and Parliament* have themselves ordered to be set up? Here, there is a consensus that the DIB must be asked for its opinion before the file is set up and must have the same right of control as on all other files, but that it *cannot be given a veto* against its own Government (as it has in Denmark).

Another question concerns the setting up of *very large files comprising most of the population*. This has been a subject of concern since the beginning of data legislation. It will probably be solved by setting up one single personal file for the whole population, from which other, smaller files can update such information as they may legally need — addresses, civil status, personal identifiers and a few other data.

As for *personal identifiers,* Prime Minister Falldin promised that this would be gone into very thoroughly and their use curtailed. The Committee set an expert to find out the consequences of abolishing the single personal identifier used in Sweden since 1949. The answer was that this would make for a great deal of trouble, because then everybody would have to keep track of not one number, but several, identifying him in various circumstances. It would on the other hand do little good in preventing files from different sources being run together to provide complete dossiers, because one can identify people to an extent of about 90 — 95% with ordinary identifiers such as name, age and addresses. I should perhaps add that running two files together to make one of them, in Sweden requires new and explicit permission from the DIB.

The Committee, however, proposed that personal identifiers may not be used on the outside of letters or other missives, in such a way as to cause annoyance.

I now come to one of the questions which have stirred up most passions in the Swedish data debate: *data for social research, and for statistics.* Researchers in these subjects, and in medicine, have in fact been the ones who have complained most loudly about the Data Act, far more than government agencies or private corporations, who have mostly kept their sufferings to themselves.

Social scientists have in fact demanded to be exempt from the Data Act and be allowed to compile their files without any authorisation by the DIB. Their arguments are that the permissions take too much time, are too costly, and constitute a kind of censorship on research.

The DIB and the committee answer that the DIB is now giving permissions much more quickly, that it might be possible to let scientists off the costs entirely, but that research in social science and in medicine often consists in gathering *the most sensitive data imaginable,* often about people who are quite unable to defend themselves, and that *someone has to look after their interests.*

The DIB has very seldom forbidden any such file outright, but they have often imposed conditions, in the interests of the subjects of the research. As a matter of fact, these conditions do not measure up in stringency to the ethical codes which some bodies of researchers in Sweden and abroad have imposed on themselves.

One may of course very well ask: is the DIB really the best forum for looking after the privacy of the interviews or the patients? And one may wish to propose some other kind of machinery for deciding what is in the best interest of the parties studied, and the parties studying them. Some kind of ethical board might be envisaged. What is impossible is to let researchers handle data on, for instance, cancer, abortions, child battering and mental health under no control at all.

It would possibly be fatal to research itself in the long run because of the resulting lack of confidence of the public.

This debate is going on at the moment more hotly than ever and there will be much more of it before we can finally agree on how far social science should be let off the hook.

Another very ticklish point the Committee has to answer is this: should the Data Act and the DIB consider anything *besides* integrity, when giving or withholding permission? Should they also consider whether the file in question is *very necessary or desirable* for public or private reasons, and let this influence their judgement? The Committee would like to let the Government take the burden of deciding in those cases, where there is a strong argument for a file which is definitely dangerous to privacy. There would perhaps be a hundred, perhaps five hundred such cases a year. No cabinet would like to be burdened with them. But the Data Act is aimed only at integrity, nothing else. Quis custodiet ipsos custodes, if I may so express myself?

I am afraid the list I am giving you will seem to jump about from one ice floe to another. Well, so it does, because computers come into every compartment of life, politics and business, and some of them catch the politicians' eyes more than others. You will have to bear with me. Some of your own ice-floes may never surface at all, I am sorry to say.

The next one I will jump on is the question of *manual systems*, or on the other hand systems as far beyond computers as those are beyond Hollerith machines. Here, the Committee has a mandate and will look into it. In certain cases, such as that of credit bureaux, Swedish law embraces manual systems, too. It has also been a worry from the beginning of the Data Act that technical development might leave it behind with the speed of light. What about microfiches, what about lasers and holograms, what about Viewdata, what about computerised newspaper, computerised mail services, the wired city?

It is the ambition of the present Committee to look into as much as possible of future developments and try to write the Act so that it will not too quickly become obsolete. One way is to define "information" or "public information" in such a way as to include everything from the Gutenberg age onwards. This brings us into particular difficulties with the Swedish concept of *public access*. At what point in time and space is information liable to public access, when it cannot be handled manually but only read by electronic instruments?

This question of public access is one which the Committee will address somewhat later on, but we will do it in a broad and imaginative way. Our point of departure is that computer technology actually opens up *new efficient ways* of utilizing the principle of public access to public records. We will have to find ways of giving the public means of really finding and using the information stored in public data banks, and to do this not only to the already information-rich, but to all segments of the populations. "People's computers" in public libraries and communal centers will have to be studied.

From the legislator's point of view, this will open up new conflicts between the *right to access* and *the right to privacy*. We have one such already with us, which the Committee is devoting a great deal of though to: the *right of using public records for commercial purposes*.

Very many organisations want to use various kinds of public data, for selling, marketing, propaganda or other purposes. They may be commercial, or religious, or political, or of other kinds. Citizens may feel that this use encroaches on their privacy, perhaps even more if the use is *not* commercial, but connected with the spreading of ideas.

Different laws apply to these data, according to whether they are *personal or not*. Names, addresses and personal identifiers, perhaps classed according to age or income (which is another public fact in Sweden, as you know!) can be bought, but can also be refused by the government agency in question, without reference to the DIB. The criterion is whether the release of these data is likely to hurt the individual whom they concern.

There is thus a precedent here for giving the interests of the individual and his privacy more weight than the equally legal right of access. But when it comes to the other sort of data, which are *not* personal, this latter right should take precedence. However, it is not easy to say *in what form exactly* the computerized data are public. Are you allowed to get, or buy, the data in written or in taped form? Can you ask for them on your own terminal? Can you ask the government agency to set up a new programme to organize data in a new way, or can you only ask them to use the programmes they have already got for their own use? And how much can they reasonably ask you to pay for their trouble?

We are considering these questions and are groping for answers. For my own part, I would stress that there are always *strong economic advantages and disadvantages* connected with having or not having access to public data in easily usable form. And the easier it becomes to use them for an enlightened public debate about what the rulers are doing, the easier it also becomes to use them for egoistic or group-egoistic purposes. The Swedish laws about public access were originally formulated 200 years ago, to serve the first purpose; they are now more and more being put to the second use. They will also more and more benefit rich organisations and consequently dis-benefit the poorer ones, whether they be corporations, trade unions, churches, or women's organisations.

This is one of our worst headaches and I can only describe it to you, not give any solution.

The kinds of data envisaged by the law about public access are of course not the ones that concern people's health, poverty, crimes, alcoholism, and such other data to be found in the banks of the welfare services. These are not public, at least not generally and in principle. But they have their own dangers, and the Committee had to look at those too.

The important aspect here is that of the use and exactitude of so-called "soft data". Soft data means, in this context, data which look like facts but are actually judgements, made by one human being about another human being. An enticing quality of automatically produced data is that they so often give the impression of being much more precise than they are, or than manually produced data.

This has nothing to do with computer technology, as every computer buff is eager to point out. It has to do with psychology, and particularly with bureaucratic psychology. One has to take it into account just the same. "The computer has said so, so it must be true, and anyway we can't change it—" how many times have we been told that by government and by business?

I have myself put forward certain ideas on how to make soft data safer to use;

— judgements about one human being by another should not be entered into a file without provision for alternative judgement from other persons and/or the individual concerned.

— a judgement should never be forced into a yes/no formula, but there should always be a possibility to express uncertainty or a completely different alternative.

— the person entering soft data in a personal file should be allowed to state that these data must never be used except in the original context.

- any judgements of this kind should always stay accompanied by the name and/or function of the person who originally made them.
- the coding system itself, i.e. what kind of questions should be asked and not asked, should be the subject of negotiations between the group of people to be described (patients, prisoners, welfare recipients etc.) and the group of people describing them.

These may be counsels of perfection, or perfectly dystopian ones, according to your views. But one would achieve a tolerable approximation of this control from below, if everybody has a *right to know* where there is a file on him, to *read* it, to *correct* it, and to have the correction *entered* not only in the original file but in *every daughter file*, and there can be many of them.

This is already law in Sweden, and we hope soon to have one which makes it mandatory on the keeper of a credit information bureau to inform the people on his files, not only *that* someone has asked about them and what information has been given out, but also *who* actually asked about them.

The Data Law Committee has added to these safeguards a proposed new paragraph in the Data Law about soft data, saying that the Board must especially take note of whether a register includes personal information which constitutes a judgement or appraisal of the registered person.

One last practical question which I hinted at earlier: what part should the *trade unions* play in deciding about *personnel files* in their employers' keep? This is one of the few points where the Committee was divided. All five political parties are represented in it, which means that it is one of the few where the small Communist party has a representative. This party has been very active in the data debate and has many opinions of its own.

In this particular matter, they argue that personnel files are so important that the trade unions should have absolute veto against any such they do not like.

The rest of us, and the DIB, argue that personal integrity is best taken care of by the agency specialized on this issue, that the DIB would not dream of deciding without first hearing what the trade unions say, that in one or two cases already,the trade unions of different workers in the same corporation have come to different conclusions, and that the new Swedish laws about workers' participation go so far that they will take care of anything the DIB may miss.

I think personally that this is just the first of many issues where *privacy* will prove to go *far beyond its first brief* to protect well-to-do individuals in their sheltered homes.

The trade unions, in their commentary to the paper, have stressed that the workers must have a strong influence on all personal files about themselves, and that all measurements of individual work quality must be regarded as extremely sensitive data. This would mean that they might not be allowed in a register except in very exceptional circumstances.

Finally, the Committee cast a look *outside Sweden.* Computer networks go far beyond national frontiers, and economic co-operation between countries and continents needs a lot of data and a lot of computers. National computer laws which contradict each other may strangle much necessary business. Swedes are eager that they should not.

But our present Data Act says, for instance, that you may not take Swedish personal files out of Sweden without express permission, this for the reason that we do not really trust the Data Acts in other countries, or because we understand that there are none at all. So we feel unprotected in those countries with our data — like walking down Fifth Avenue in our underwear.

To feel better dressed, we work hard for international data conventions. This is not precisely the job of the Committee, but it works in close contact with such bodies in or outside Sweden who do try to harmonise Nordic, European or OECD laws. Any changes that will have to be made in Swedish laws to help such harmonising, will go through the Committee.

Transborder data flow is chiefly about *economic data* not personal ones, but they are often difficult to tell apart. Think of the different credit bureau legislations, for instance. Or how international agreements on taxation and pensions should be implemented. Or the different laws that may rule bank transactions in different countries.

But the danger for privacy and integrity in one country of being abused by data banks located in a "data haven" outside it, are not to be dismissed. The kind of advertisement or propaganda that one country bans, may be sent in from another. Or data profiles and dossiers — what we call in Sweden "data shadows" — may be built up abroad, for instance by a multi-national corporation, and used in a country where such files are forbidden.

Not all such abuses can be prevented by international agreements, but certainly some of them. It would be a happy thing if the laws could be there almost as quickly as the criminals, or even a little earlier.

Finally, one word about *privacy.* Just like every other committee on this delicate subject, our Committee decided early on that it could not define privacy. I should like now to be allowed a few personal words on this vexed subject.

I think we will always find ourselves in a deadlock, as long as we content ourselves with what I call a "concentric" model of privacy. I mean this mental picture of the individual in the middle of a huge circle. Close to him, there is a very small circle which encloses his "privacy". Within that space, he is protected, but as soon as he steps out of it, the strobe lights play on him and he is totally visible. The futile and dangerous question then is: *where precisely* do we draw this inner circle? That question can never be answered.

I would propose a different model. I did not invent it, but I like it.

The first model made the citizen unfree, because somebody else then decides from the outside where the space of his free actions ceases. The model I propose carves up the whole big circle outside his "privacy" into segments, each sector representing one particular part or facet of society as it meets him. Now, in each sector it is to the interest of the citizen to be treated with the help of certain bits of information about him, but not all the bits there are.

He wants to be treated differently according to whether he is at the moment acting as tax-payer, father, voter, school-child, prisoner, worker, patient, client, customer etc. In every specific role he wants to be identified by certain data, but not necessarily by the same data in the next role he plays.

Now, in every one of these sectors there must of course be a different mix between the interests of the citizen, his co-citizens, and the state. They will be very different indeed if he, as a taxpayer, must be completely transparent to his masters, or if he, as a newly released prisoner, can expect a decent veil on his past before his employer and his new fellow-workers. What I do say is that this sectoral model makes it easier to discuss *how to weigh* these different interests against each other.

This would mean *an operational definition of privacy,* and could be expressed as the right to decide (or help decide) what information about oneself one wishes to release in each special situation. To call one role more "private" than another is to obscure the issue. As citizens, we want control over *all* our roles. As private persons, we may want less privacy than anywhere — in relation to one, or very few, chosen persons.

The right to our information tracks throughout the world.

The right to know where they go, and who collects them. And the right to know in return as much as possible about our masters, the information-capitalists. That is what I think a good Data Act and Privacy Act should aim at.

Annex: A summary of privacy legislation in the USA by Trudy Hayden

Federal and state legislatures in the United States have been experimenting with various forms of data protection legislation over a decade. The first major step was the Federal Freedom of Information Act (FOIA)(1), which is not, strictly speaking, a "privacy" law at all, but rather, an access law. The FOIA permits members of the public to have access to information and documents maintained by federal agencies. It was originally intended to be used by journalists, researchers, and others with an interest in matters of public policy, to obtain information explaining what government agencies were doing and why. But with the revelations of the Watergate years about massive governmental prying and spying and dossier collection on the lives of individuals, people discovered that they could use the FOIA to get their *own* files from government agencies, and the FOIA thus became a kind of privacy law. So much so, in fact, that at one time the FBI was over a year behind in processing applications by citizens for access to their dossiers, even though the law states that access must be granted within ten business days.

There is no doubt that the growing use of the FOIA for personal data purposes created the necessary political impetus for passage of the Privacy Act of 1974. The Privacy Act (2) establishes an individual right of access to personal records maintained by federal government agencies. In addition, it creates a right to challenge information which the data subject believes to be incorrect, untimely, incomplete, or irrelevant, a right to prevent certain disclosures of information by the agency without the individual's authorisation, and the right to obtain from the agency a full acounting of the uses and disclosures of personal data that have been made. It also places on federal agencies which maintain personal record systems, certain duties and responsibilities in the maintenance, use and disclosure of such information (3), and establishes a reporting system whereby each agency must publish annually a full description of its personal data systems, their routine uses, any proposed new uses, and the procedures to be followed by persons who wish to examine and correct their own records.

There are three other important federal statutes dealing with the collection and uses of personal information. One, the Fair Credit Reporting Act of 1970 (FRCA)(4), deals with the activities of credit reporting or investigative reporting agencies, private sector organisations which compile and sell reports on individuals for use by creditors, insurers, employers, landlords, and other business users. The FRCA requires that a data subject be informed when a report is to be compiled, be permitted to learn the "nature and substance" of the information in his or her file, and be permitted to challenge the accuracy of the information. But the rights available to the data subject under the FRCA are circumscribed by numerous exemptions and restrictions, a result of the fact that the law was virtually written by the industry whose data practices it is purported to regulate. Repeated attempts to amend and strengthen the FRCA since 1970 have so far been unavailing.

The second is the Family Educational Rights and Privacy Act (FERPA)(5), also known as the Buckley Amendment, which pertains to education records. Under FERPA, students (or the parents of students under 18) have the right to see their own records, challenge information which they believe to be inaccurate or incomplete, and prevent disclosures for most purposes without their consent. And late last year, Congress enacted the Right to Financial Privacy Act of 1978, which prohibits federal government officials from obtaining access to a person's bank records without former legal process and prior notice (a prohibition hedged, however, by many significant exceptions).

Alongside these federal statutes, are a scattering of state laws dealing with different kinds of personal records. About ten states have passed state privacy laws modelled on the Federal Privacy Act, here regulating personal data systems maintained by agencies of state and local governments. A number of states have credit reporting acts, most of them merely repeating the provisions of the federal act, but two, in Maine and New York, provide significantly greater protections against the abuse of information by credit reporting agencies. Five states — Oregon, Maryland, Alaska, Illinois and California — have statutes limiting access by state government officials to a person's bank records. In several states, persons employed in the private sector have a statutory right of access to their own employment records. A number of states provide patients with a statutory right of access to their own medical records — though always with a long list of exemptions and caveats — and attempt to protect those records from dissemination to other parties without the patient's authorisation. A few states restrict employers' access to arrest records. Some others give the individual the statutory right to expunge the record of an arrest which did not result in a conviction.

Obviously the picture is confused: the legislatures have ventured into issues of data protection one by one, but without a clear sense of what results they hope to achieve, what balance they want to strike between personal privacy and society's need for a flow of information.

In evaluating what the legislatures have accomplished, it is necessary to appreciate the fact that the judiciary, both federal and state, have shown themselves completely insensitive to questions of information privacy. The US Supreme Court in particular has been obtusely blind, almost hostile, to arguments that certain kinds of data collection and data use can have harmful effects on the constitutional rights and civil liberties of individuals. In *Laird v. Tatum* (6), the court ruled that the army's collection of political dossiers describing how individual civilians exercised their constitutional rights to freedom of speech and association has no "chilling effect" upon the enjoyment of those rights, in other words, the knowledge that government was officially watching and recording their political activities would not make people more cautious or timid in expressing their political beliefs or taking part in political organisations. In *Paul v. Davis* (7), the court rejected the contention that a police official's dissemination of derogatory personal information (in this case false) is actionable where injury is "merely" to reputation and does not result in tangible damage, such as the loss of employment. In *US v. Miller* (8), the court ruled that a person's bank records are records of commercial transactions and belong to the bank, not to the customer, the customer can have no "reasonable expectation of privacy" in them. And in *Whalen v. Roe* (9), the court, in a unanimous decision found no threat to privacy in the mandatory collection in a computerised government databank of the records of all the patients for whom certain "dangerous" drugs are prescribed by their physicians.

For the most part, the lower federal bench and state courts have followed the lead of the US Supreme Court. A splendid exception is the state judiciary in California, which has been much more sensitive to the potential harm to personal privacy posed by massive data collection and dissemination. The California Courts, two years before the *Miller* decision had declared that because a person's bank records are the mirror of his personal life he should have some legally enforceable expectation of privacy in those records (10). (And some years later, the US Congress came to the same conclusion, enacting the Right to Financial Privacy Act of 1978 to overcome the presumption of the *Miller* decision and to create an expectation of the privacy of bank records.)

It is because the judiciary has been so slow to recognise the constitutional and civil liberties questions raised by modern methods of data collection and dissemination that the emphasis has passed to legislative action. Except where statute law, either federal or state, explicitly places certain obligations upon record keepers and explicitly gives certain rights to record subjects, individuals are left virtually without protection against the unrestricted collection and dissemination of data about them, and virtually without rights to access to and correct their own records.

It was expected that the Federal Privacy Protection Study Commission would bring some order, direction, and substance into this picture of confusion. The commission, established under the Privacy Act of 1974, carried a statutory mandate to develop the outlines of a "national information policy," specifically, to formulate concrete proposals for legislation, administrative regulation, and self-regulation of public and private data systems designed "to protect the privacy of individuals while meeting the legitimate needs of government and society for information." The seven member Commission was appointed in the summer of 1975 and delivered its Report, an 800-page tome, in July 1977. The report contains scores of proposals for action by the Congress, by the state legislatures, by government agencies and by the many organisations in the private sector which maintain and use personal information.

The Privacy Commission Report has been criticised by the privacy advocates on a number of grounds: for its fragmented style, which tends to obscure the underlying principles of information privacy and focuses attention instead on details and particulars; for an avoidance of many difficult value judgements about the uses of personal information in a democratic society, and for a rather too-gentle approach to the practices of organisations in the private sector, with respect to which the Commission relied primarily upon self-regulation rather than legislative control.

The Commission identified three major objectives fundamental to an effective data protection policy; these objectives form the basis of the Commission's recommendations for legislation or self-regulation touching more than a dozen different kinds of personal data systems (11). They are:

"To minimise intrusiveness," that is, "to create a proper balance between what an individual is expected to divulge to a record-keeping organisation and what he seeks in return." Many privacy advocates believe that the Commission's proposals in pursuit of this goal are far too timid and unlikely to produce any major changes in prevailing data collection practices either in government or in the private sector.

"To maximise fairness" that is, "to open record-keeping operations in ways that will minimise the extent to which recorded information about an individual is itself a source of unfairness in any decision about him." This principle is the basis for the many procedural recommendations in the Commission Report, the "codes of fair information practice" which the Commission outlines for each separate category of public and private data system. These codes comprise both duties of fair data collection, maintenance and use for record keepers, and rights of access, correction and "To create legitimate, enforceable expectations of confidentiality," that is "to create and define obligations with respect to the uses and disclosures that will be made of recorded information about an individual." This means, first, that the record keeper must refrain from disclosing an individual's records to others without the individual's authorisation, and second, that the individual must be provided with "standing", or a recognised legal interest in the record, which he or she can assert against an improper or unreasonable demand for disclosure.

Despite shortcomings, the Commission Report reawakened flagging interest in the subject of personal privacy and data protection, and laid out an impressive agenda for the Congress, and state legislatures, governmental agencies and private businesses and organisations. A number of important data protection bills received Congressional hearings last year, and one, the bank privacy statute, was adopted. Most of the state legislatures are considering at least one major data protection bill, some of them more. A year-long White House study of the Commission's recommendations is expected to culminate in the publication of a Presidential program on many aspects of government data collection policy some time this year. The private sector too has been spurred into some action, with many large corporations and professional and business associations re-examining their personal data practices and systems in the light of the Commission's recommendations — if only defensively, with an eye to the effects of possible statutory or regulatory restrictions.

There are quite a number of glaring problems in the state of US privacy law.

First there is still a lack of clear direction, of consensus on goals. Most of the existing laws try to make things better for the individual data subject, but do not tamper with long-established data collection and usage practices of government of business in any significant way. The approach of the legislatures has been piecemeal, and often contradictory. It must be said that the Report of the Privacy Commission, though it contains many good recommendations, does not diminish the confusion. The United States is still without a "national information policy", in that we are still undecided as to the proper balance between the right of personal privacy and the use of personal data to conduct the daily affairs of government and business. And while that indecisiveness continues, the encroachments of data collection and data use upon the right of personal privacy become even greater; some privacy advocates now wonder whether it is already too late to recapture any meaningful right of personal privacy.

Secondly, and as an extension of the first point, US data protection laws deal primarily with procedures, rather than with substance. That is, the laws give the data subjects certain rights — the right to know what records are being kept and the sources of information in those records, the right to examine and correct one's own records, the right to prevent unauthorised disclosures, and so on — and place certain obligations and responsibilities on the record keepers. But they do not address such basic questions as: What kinds of data systems, if any, ought not to exist at all? (12) What kinds of data ought not to be available or used for certain kinds of decisions? What methods of obtaining information ought not to be allowed? Existing data protection laws have a great deal to say about how data systems should be managed, but little to say about their contents or uses.

Third, many of the laws are difficult or impossible to enforce. Under the Privacy Act, the Freedom of Information Act, the Fair Credit Reporting Act, and the Right to Financial Privacy Act, and under most state protection laws, an aggrieved person may undertake a civil action to obtain his rights and perhaps recover damages for the violation of his rights. But reliance on this kind of self-help — which is beyond the financial means and emotional stamina of most ordinary people unless the stakes are very high — means that most violations will go uncorrected. There is no built-in mechanism for systematic enforcement and oversight, no responsible authority to whom aggrieved data subjects can take their complaints and entrust with the redress of wrongs. But the problem is just the opposite under the Family Educational Rights and Privacy Act. Here, there is no provision for recourse to the courts, a special office in the federal Department of Health, Education and Welfare is given powers to investigate grievances and enforce sanctions against educational institutions that fail to live up to their statutory obligations. That office, however, is remote from the daily lives of most citizens, slow to move, and hampered in its enforcement efforts by the law's provision of a draconian sanction, the total withdrawal of federal funds from the offending institution, which makes it highly unlikely to be invoked. (No one seriously expects that all federal money will be taken away from a secondary school because the school has refused to let a few students' parents see their records, or has released some records without proper authorisation.)

Thus the problem of effective enforcement, within the reach of the ordinary data subject, has yet to be solved. Under the new California privacy act, a state fair information practices board with some enforcement powers has been established, its experiences and effectiveness will be instructive. The Privacy Commission has proposed a federal Fair Information Practices Board, with oversight rather than enforcement powers, if enacted, this experiment too, could prove instructive. But it is frankly difficult to envision any single enforcement mechanism that can reach the many data systems of varying character and function that touch the life of each individual, and that can give accessible, simple, effective procedures for enforcement and oversight of privacy laws.

Fourth, the laws are based on what the Privacy Commission called a "file-cabinet mentality." There is a serious question whether existing, and proposed future data protection laws and the assumptions upon which they are based cannot be rendered obsolete or merely irrelevant by computer technology. For example, the Privacy Act does not prevent the widespread matching of whole data systems by computer, under federal and state programs to verify eligibility for public assistance benefits, even though this involves the pooling of personal data in tax, employment, public assistance, unemployment compensation, and other massive data systems. Once this information has been shared from computer to computer, the barriers between data systems which are so carefully protected by the Privacy Act are useless.

Fifth, there is the problem of consent. Privacy statutes all employ the concept of the data subject's consent to disclosures of information from a personal data system. But in many, if not most situations, the giving of consent is an empty ritual, satisfying the letter of the law but expressing no freedom of choice on the individual's part. If a government agency or private business simply refuses to deal with the individual without a particular item of data or without, in many instances, carte blanche to examine certain kinds of records in their entirety, the "consent" which the person signs is in fact meaningless. This brings the issue back, once again, to the substantive question of how we use personal data in a democratic society that places values on the right of personal privacy.

Notes

1. 5 USC 552, enacted 1966, effective 1967, amendments enacted in 1974, effective 1975.

2. 5 USC 552a.

3. For example: an agency must obtain data directly from the data subject to the fullest extent possible; an agency must take all reasonable steps to ensure that the data in its personal record systems are accurate, timely, relevant and complete; an agency may collect only such personal data as are relevant to its statutorily authorised functions and duties; personal data may be disclosed only to those employees and officials of the agency who need it for their official duties; an agency must log each disclosure of personal data to a party outside the agency; if the agency disclose any information whose accuracy, timeliness, relevance, or completeness have been challenged by the data subject, it must either amend the record as requested by the subject or include in the record a statement of the subject's version of the facts.

4. 15 USC 1681

5. 20 USC 1232g.

6. 408 US 1 (1972).

7. 424 US 693 (1976).

7. 425 US 435 (1976).

9. 429 US 589 (1977).

10. *Burrows v. Superior Court*, 13 Cal. 3d 238 (1974).

11. The commission's specific proposals cover credit records, bank records, mailing lists, insurance records, employment records, medical records, the practices of investigative reporting agencies, government access to private personal records, education records, public assistance and social services records, tax records and the use of personal data in research and statistical studies, as well as revisions of the Privacy Act and uses of the Social Security number as a universal identifier. The subject of criminal justice information systems was not contained in the Commission's statutory mandate.

12. An important exception is that provision of the Privacy Act which forbids federal agencies to maintain data systems containing information about individuals' political and religious beliefs or activities, unless they are explicitly authorised to do so by law. No serious attempt has yet been made to enforce this provision, nor can this be done until Congress deals with the subject of the proper limits of political surveillance and investigative activities by federal agencies.

Annex; A summary of international developments by Russell Pipe

It has been claimed, and rightly so, that data protection and freedom of information are sister principles, the former opening personal records to the individual data subject and the latter making available government records in general to public inspection. In many ways data protection legislation is the more avant garde — by establishing rights of access to personal dossiers held by both government and private organisations, applying to manual as well as computerised information, and requiring rules of relevance, prudence and accuracy in the maintenance of materials relating to individuals. Even in the United States and Sweden freedom of information statutes fall short of these bold accomplishments. Therefore we should salute data protection as a hallmark of making trust a two-way street for all organisations holding significant economic and social information.

The purpose of this paper is to briefly outline the national and international status of data protection which hopefully is in large part accomplished by the series of tables which are presented.

Long Lasting Impacts

In brief, I see the coming year as a period for implementation of several laws approved in 1978, especially by Denmark, France and Norway and the enactment of similar statutes by parliaments in Belgium, Finland, Luxembourg, The Netherlands and Spain. These laws are expected to follow present trends for an omnibus approach which imposes similar rules on the public and private sectors, establishes independent regulatory authorities, applies to ADP but includes "sensitive manual records," and conditions foreign data flows on equivalent protection.

It is particularly exciting to note that data protection is unlikely to be a fleeting public issue, even though it is grudgingly accepted in some government quarters. There seem to be four main driving forces to legislation beyond general public and political support:

1. Constitutional rights to information privacy bring a new and formidable force propelling legislative developments. The Spanish constitution contains such a provision (Article 18) and privacy rights are among the items to be incorporated in revised Belgian and Swiss constitutions. The Austrians used a constitutional mandate to justify its strong data protection act. The Portugese constitution (Article 35) is explicit in granting information privacy rights: 'All citizens shall have the right to information on the contents of data banks concerning them and on the use for which it is intended. They shall be entitled to require the said contents to be corrected and brought up to date.'

2. It has confirmed the legislative approach taken by other European countries in terms of an omnibus scope imposing rules on public and private sectors alike, called for an independent regulatory authority, applied rules to automated records but not fully excluded manual files, and recognised the need for equivalent protection of foreign stored data.

3. It sent a message to non-European countries, especially Australia and New Zealand that Anglo-Saxon law can comfortably accommodate the data protection concept as formulated in Continental legislation.

There are many comparable features between the Committee's suggestions and the newest national law, the Austrian Data Protection Act. The Austrian law applies to the following:

— public and private sectors
— EDP and some manual files
— creates a regulatory agency
— establishes a registry of personal files, requires that personal data be collected by lawful and fair means, kept accurate, confidentiality maintained, secondary use controlled, external transfers logged and security measures adopted
— sets penalties for violations

— Gives data subjects rights to be informed or otherwise notified of personal data stored, access to their own files, and ability to correct or have erroneous information deleted; and
— conditions transborder data flows

The major difference between the Committee's conclusions and those of the Austrian parliament are the inclusion of legal persons (companies) by the Austrian and a greater role in manual files. The UK approach would add greater specificity to record-keeping requirements by creating some 50 Codes of Practice for various record-keeping sectors.

International Organisation Developments

Several international organisations have become involved in the data protection issue since the late 1960s. The council of Europe perceived data protection as an important dimension of the European Convention on Human Rights (Articles 8 and 10) e.g. assuring rights of individuals vis-a-vis automatic processing of personal data. Initially, the Council of Europe's Directorate on Legal Affairs prepared recommendations to member states for the adoption of data protection laws in the public and private sectors. Since 1976 it has been mandated to prepare a convention or treaty for the Protection of Individuals with Regard to Automated Data Files.

A Committee of Experts was formed to draft the convention and is now involved in final preparations before submission to the Committee on Legal Co-operation. The main provisions of the text (Table V) have been agreed upon but the conflict of laws section, the convention's impact on present national law, and a number of substantive points remain to be resolved. A final text is expected sometime in 1979.

The Organisation for Economic Co-operation and Development (OECD) began consideration of EDP in public administration and framing policies for their efficient and effective application. Because improving economic, scientific and technological co-operation is fundamental to its charter, the OECD has not embarked on the preparation of a binding international convention. Instead, working groups representing the 24 member countries have considered various approaches to data protection.

A major conference on Transborder Data Flows and Protection of Privacy was held in Vienna in September 1977 which confirmed the international importance of efforts to harmonise national legislation. This resulted in the forming of an Expert Group on Transborder Data Barriers and Protection of Privacy in 1978. This group was commissioned to prepare Draft Guidelines on Basic Rules Governing the Transborder Flow and Protection of Personal Data. Its mandate calls for submission of a text before July 1979 to the OECD Council of Ministers. A second meeting of the group, under the chairmanship of Mr. Justice Kirby of Australia was held in December and two concluding sessions are scheduled. Although the Guidelines will be a non-binding agreement, they will be addressed to the member governments with a certain moral force for implementation. The OECD as an organisation of the free world's democracies has a special interest in multilateral co-operation to foster the free flow of information, open commercial markets, fair competition and strengthening human rights; upon which the guidelines will be formulated.

Since 1974 the European Parliament has demonstrated concern for data protection within its nine member states. A Subcommittee on Data Processing and Individual Rights has considered the issue and will submit recommendations to the Legal Affairs Committee and full parliament in the spring. Presently, the parliament exerts only moral suasion on the Commission, the Executive organ of the European Economic Communities (EEC). When a popularly elected parliament is seated next fall there are signs that data protection advocates may become more vocal and have greater impact on EEC institutions. The Commission itself seems to be awaiting some concrete results from the Council of Europe and OECD before defining a possible directive for its members.

Table 1

Status of Data Protection Legislation

Country	National	Sub-National	Reports
Australia		L	RP
Austria	L		R
Belgium	P		
Canada	L	L	R
Denmark	L		R
Finland			RP
France	L		R
Germany	L	LP	R
Greece			
Iceland			RP
Ireland			
Italy			RP
Japan			RP
Luxembourg	P		
Netherlands	P		R
New Zealand			RP
Norway	L		R
Portugal			
Spain	P		R
Sweden	L		R
Switzerland		L	RP
United Kingdom			R
United States	LP	LP	R
Yugoslavia			RP

Source: Transnational Data Report

Code: L = Law Adopted
             P = Legislation in Parliament
             R = Government Report Prepared
             RP = Government Report in Preparation

Table II

Basic Requirements of National Data Protection Legislation

Scope of Legislation

Central Government Only: Canada[1], United States[1]

Public and Private Sectors (Separate instruments): Denmark

Public and Private Sectors (One instrument): Austria, Belgium,France, Germany, Luxembourg, The Netherlands, Norway, Spain, Sweden, United Kingdom

Application to Record—Keeping Methods

EDP Only: Belgium, Luxembourg

EDP and Files Linked to Manual Files: Denmark, France, Sweden, United Kingdom

EDP and Manual Files[2] Austria, Canada, Germany The Netherlands, Norway, Spain, United States.

Enforcement Mechanism

Supervisory Authority: Austria, Belgium, Germany, Luxembourg

Regulation/Inspection Agency: Austria, Belgium, Canada, Denmark, France, The Netherlands, Norway, Spain, Sweden, United Kingdom

Judicial Remedies: United States

1 State of Provincial Statutes Enacted

2 May be Conditioned on Sensitivity of Manual Files

Source:- Transnational Data Report

Table III

Data Protection Obligations for Controllers of Personal Data

Status as at January 1979	Austria	Belgium	Canada	Denmark	France	Germany	Luxembourg	Netherlands	Norway	Spain	Sweden	United Kingdom	United States
Licensing of Personal Registers													
Central Government...........		Y		X	X			X	Y	X	X	X	
States, Provinces, Localities....		Y		X					Y	X	X	X	
Private Sector...............		Y		Y					Y	X	X	X	
Registration of Personal Registers													
Central Government...........	X	Y	X	X	X	X	X	X	X	X	X	X	X
States, Provinces, Localities....	X	Y		X	X	Z		X	X	X	X	X	Z
Private Sector...............		Y		Y	X	Y		X	X	X	X	X	
1. Collection by fair and lawful means...................	X	X		X	X				X			X	X
2. Maintenance of Accuracy...	X	X	X	X	X	X	X	X	X	X	X	X	X
3. Appropriate and Relevant..	X	X	X	X	X	X	X	X	X	X	X	X	X
4. Confidentiality, Prevent Misuse	X	X	X	X	X	X	X	X	X	X	X	X	X
5. Sensitive Data Restricted...		X		X	X			X	X	X	X		
6. Secondary Use Controlled..	X		X	X				X	X	X	X	X	X
7. Retention Time Limited....				X	X	X				X		X	
8. External Transfer Logged...	X	X	X	X		X			Y		X		X
9. Security Measures Necessary	X	X	X	X	X	X	X	X	X	X	X	X	X
10. Penalties for Violation.....	X	X	X	X	X	X	X	X	X	X	X	X	X
11. Transborder Data Flow Conditions...............	X			X	X	X	X	X	X	X	X	X	

Y Partial, usually according to sensitivity or specific legislative provision
Z Subject to state or provincial law

Table IV

Rights of Data Subjects

	Austria	Belgium	Canada	Denmark	France	Germany	Luxembourg	Netherlands	Norway	Spain	Sweden	United Kingdom	United States
1. Be informed of the obligation or freedom to divulge information					X	X					X		
2. To ascertain or be notified of personal data storage	X	X	X	X	X	X		X	X	X	X	X	X
3. To access one's own file[a]	X	X	X	Y	X	X	X	X	X	X	X	Y	X
4. To request correction or deletion of information	X	X	X	X	X	X	X	X	X	X	Z	X	X

a   medical records may be accessed through a physician

Y   partial or conditional

Z   Data Act imposes only an obligation that records be kept accurate

Source: Transnational Data Report

COUNCIL OF EUROPE DRAFT CONVENTION[1] FOR THE
Protection of Individuals with Regard to Automated Data Files
Outline of Main Provisions

I.   Applies to automatic processing of personal data in the public and private sectors.

II.   Prescribes minimum rules for data protection:

     A.   Collection by fair and lawful means;

     B.   Accurate, complete and relevant;

     C.   Use only for a declared purpose;

     D.   No recording of data relevant to religion, political or other opinion, racial origin, or leading to discrimination;

     E.   Recipients specified in advance;

     F.   Appropriate security measures;

     G.   Subject to know existence of data, use and recipients;

     H.   Rights to amend and correct data; and

     I.   Statistical data maintained in aggregated form.

III.   Provides remedies for data subject when data is processed or maintained abroad.

IV.   Establishes co-operation between national data protection authorities.

V.   Forms standing consultative committee of signatory States to monitor convention, receive reports and propose modifications.

---

1.   A Committee of Experts on Data Protection is responsible for the preparation of a draft text to be submitted to the Committee on Legal Co-operation during 1979.

APPENDIX A

A SUMMARY OF EVIDENCE TO THE DATA PROTECTION COMMITTEE

1. Government Departments

Central Computer Agency	Ministry of Agriculture Fisheries & Food	(Cabinet Office) Central Statistics Office	Ministry of Defence	
		This Proposal was "welcomed"		*Para 34:* *Existence and purpose of information systems holding personal data in computers, use made of data and which interests have access to be publicly known.*
		Because statistics are anonymous, "statistical use" should be acceptable description of purpose.	Generally complied with. Exceptions:- - Inland Revenue for tax purposes - security services have access - data transferred for stats.	*Para 34:* *Information not to be used for purpose other than that for which given without consent of subject or other authorised justification.*
				Para 34: *Only personal Information necessary for declared purposes should be collected.*
				Para 34: *Operator of system to be responsible for ensuring accuracy and relevance of information.*
	Very concerned at cost of this. e.g. 200,000 farmers prepare annual returns for agricultural census.	Not feasible for statistics because of cost and difficulty of establishing accuracy.	Very heavy administration and cost burden in case of servicemen if implemented.	*Para 34:* *Subject to be able to check relevance and accuracy and correct.*
		Unnecessary, costly, if not impossible for statistics.		*Para 34:* *Subject to be able to find out what done with information and to whom given.*
		Want to keep it for historical research		*Para 34:* *Information to be kept only for as long as it is needed.*
		Statistics revealing identifiable information should not be published or released outside Govt. departments unless subject consents or independent endorsement of no harm. But exceptions.		*Para 34:* *Safeguards needed to ensure statistics presented in way which doesn't reveal details of identifiable individual.*
	p.37 (2) preferred. p.37 (1) too authoritarian. What is registered anyway, every task processed?	Apart from cost considerations, p.37 (2) preferred	Want working arrangement with DPA to obviate outside supervision.	*Para 37(1) - registration/ licensing or* *Para 37(2) - information gathering, investigating complaints and publishing findings*
Definition based on hardware characteristics inappropriate.	Any hardware capable of reading, processing or storing data and producing output for transfer to human readable media.	Agree with CCA		*What is a computer?*
Suggest: "information about an individual that contains his name or identifying particulars which allows identification by person with access to record".	Must include any information which could be embarrassing to subject if divulged.	Any information containing particulars allowing identification by a person with access to records. Similar information on families should be personal.		*How should personal information be defined?*
No clear answer. May be said they are not analogous to individuals. On the other hand associations having a business in agricultural sector	Yes. Note: preponderance of one-man			*Protection for associations and corporate bodies.*

Department of Education and Science	Department of Employment (Incl. Manpower Services Commission, Employment Service Agency, Training Services Agency, Health & Safety Commission & Executive)	DHSS	Inland Revenue	
	Acceptable if existence and purpose merely published. Not a problem either if individuals to be notified (i.e. individuals with whom DE deals directly). Problems if info. supplied by 3rd party.	Leaflets could be prepared but objections to giving information on enquiry.	Agrees.	*Para 34:* *Existence and purpose of information systems holding personal data in computers, use made of data and which interests have access to be publicly known.*
Potential linkage of FESR with other records held by DES on usage of education system.	States that this is general position. However there are exceptions e.g. claimants addresses to police, other (unspecified) to local authorities and researchers.	Agrees in principle but exceptions when it may be unnecessary, impracticable or unwarranted to seek consent.	Appear to be constraints on Inland Revenue in this respect.	*Para 34:* *Information not to be used for purpose other than that for which given without consent of subject or other authorised justification.*
		'The department's activities in the collection of information are limited to the administration of the S of Ss responsibilities'.	Purpose must be wide enough to cover all Inland Revenue's functions.	*Para 34:* *Only personal Information necessary for declared purposes should be collected.*
	'Operator' may be hard to define, e.g. DE and DHSS use some of other's computers. Requirement that operator ensure accuracy is impossibly onerous.	Cannot be. e.g. checking of input from subjects?		*Para 34:* *Operator of system to be responsible for ensuring accuracy and relevance of information.*
FESR and USR open to subjects for inspection. Little use made of this. School records: LEA'S responsibility.	Unnecessarily burdensome. Note problem of charging unemployed for print-outs. Problems with confidential or medical information on files.	Scale of this daunting for DHSS. Also risks to privacy i.e. third party seeing record.	Opposed on cost grounds.	*Para 34:* *Subject to be able to check relevance and accuracy and correct.*
	Want DHSS, DE, ESA to be regarded as administrative entity for this purpose. Information exchange for administration purposes should not have to be reported.	Agreed in principle, but in practice exceptions.	Not at a detailed level.	*Para 34:* *Subject to be able to find out what done with information and to whom given.*
	This is practice in DE for most data, but may be many years. Health information on file till death. Cohort analysis follows through ident. individuals for many years.	Agreed	Agree (if only to release tapes for further use).	*Para 34:* *Information to be kept only for as long as it is needed.*
Department has not issued guidance to research councils.	Said to be practice	Normal government statistical practice followed.	Complied with. Do not like the idea of separate index:- no need: added costs.	*Para 34:* *Safeguards needed to ensure statistics presented in way which doesn't reveal details of identifiable individual.*
	Given no. of systems - 10,000 in 1975, checking for p.37(1) vast task. p.37(2) - essentially need to police systems and p.37(2) falls short, but would re-assure.		Natural choice for government departments is p.37(2). They are used to parliamentary commissioner. Anyway its inconceivable that a licence be withheld.	*Para 37(1) - registration/ licensing or* *Para 37(2) - information gathering, investigating complaints and publishing findings*
				What is a computer?
				How should personal information be defined?
				Protection for associations and corporate bodies.

Northern Ireland Office	Office of Population Census and Surveys	Scottish Home and Health Department	
Stats. unit:- compliance easy in most cases, but NIO would not want publicity for same systems. (police security)	O.K. at general level, but absurd to give individuals full details of what to be done with census information.		*Para 34:* *Existence and purpose of information systems holding personal data in computers, use made of data and which interests have access to be publicly known.*
Consents should not be needed for use for statistics or administration purposes. Do not hamper linkage for research.	Should be no bar to statistics uses.		*Para 34:* *Information not to be used for purpose other than that for which given without consent of subject or other authorised justification.*
	In statistics and research studies information may be collected without a prior certainty it is relevant. So 'necessary' must not be too narrow.		*Para 34:* *Only personal Information necessary for declared purposes should be collected.*
Unacceptable in case of statistics.	Some inaccuracy is tolerable in statistics systems.		*Para 34:* *Operator of system to be responsible for ensuring accuracy and relevance of information.*
Completely unworkable for statistics.	Unacceptable because of costs, practical difficulties, dangers of providing print-outs.		*Para 34:* *Subject to be able to check relevance and accuracy and correct.*
	Excessively costly, and thought demands would be insignificant in volume.		*Para 34:* *Subject to be able to find out what done with information and to whom given.*
O.K. in principle but statistics unit want to hang on to information in case of unforeseen uses.	Demographic and medical research covers long periods. Public Records Office envisage indefinite retention of some records.		*Para 34:* *Information to be kept only for as long as it is needed.*
Already exist.	Accepted, but tricky subject. No ultimate guarantee possible of non-identification.		*Para 34:* *Safeguards needed to ensure statistics presented in way which doesn't reveal details of identifiable individual.*
Statistics unit:- no preference. Dept. of Civil Service NI:- DPA should have powers to investigate complaints, including right of access to information and publish findings. i.e. 'ombudsman' powers.	p.37(2) a gradualist approach. Possibly later a registration/licensing system.	Suggest 3rd possibility i.e. registration and powers to investigate. But p.37(2) preferable to p.37(1).	*Para 37(1) - registration/licensing or* *Para 37(2) - information gathering, investigating complaints and publishing findings*
No good trying to define in hardware terms.		Support CCA views. Avoid definition connected to current technology.	*What is a computer?*
	Information about households and families should be included.	Support CCA but include families, households.	*How should personal information be defined?*
Case to protect bodies or associations as well as individuals is "indisputable".		Add to CCA points:- standards for firms need to dovetail with statistics of Trade	*Protection for associations and corporate bodies.*

Central Computer Agency	Ministry of Agriculture Fisheries & Food	(Cabinet Office) Central Statistics Office	Ministry of Defence	
Distinguish hearsay from third parties and information transferred under statute or between departments or public authorities. Perhaps first category need verification before inclusion or 'labelling' to indicate source. Costs of labeling formidable.	Almost all input from subject. Strict control over release to third parties (including government departments).	Transfer from department which collected information should be authorisable by Minister, if information required solely for statistics purposes.	Special considerations required for information transferred for security purposes.	*Transfer of information by third parties and not subject in person.*
				Exceptions to disclosure for medical and social work records.
Employees should be able to check non-management information	PRISM Print out issued to subject regularly. Management information not available.		Para 34 objectives of little relevance. Management and security information not available to subject.	*Personnel records*
Separate submission made by Lord Chancellor's Department		Undesirable if incorrect statistics information could form grounds for defamation.		*Qualified privilege available to computer users (and informants).*
Over all individuals, associations, bodies in U.K. handling personal information, subject to limited exceptions consistent with public interest.				*DPA's Jurisdiction~*
Through minister to Parliament (On appointment of schedule 1 of EPA 75)				*To whom DPA answerable.*
Not if para 37(2) form accepted. If licensing/registration, then on point of principle to minister on point of law to courts.				*DPA decisions appealable.*
			Want exemption for security information including that held at defence contractors.	*Exemptions for police, national security.*
EEC seeking harmonisation of laws.		Transfers to international agencies on assurance for statistics purposes. Also disclosures to EEC agencies. Provisions of Treaty of Rome for confidentiality		*Trans-border data flow.*
	Difficult to quantify.			*Costs.*
				Legislation to cover manual systems also.

	Department of Education and Science	Department of Employment (incl. Manpower Services Commission, Employment Service Agency, Training Services Agency, Health & Safety Commission and Executive)	DHSS	Inland Revenue
Transfer of information by third parties and not subject in person.	"Labelling" unnecessary for DES records: LEA's discretion generally.	Note: Health & Safety Commission & Executive have wide powers to extract information.	Principle is that in social security administration, personal information for social security purposes only. But exceptions e.g. addresses to police, local authorities.	C f CCA on this. Want second category to include information from the employers.
Exceptions to disclosure for medical and social work records.			Yes - on subject access, control of disclosure and knowing what is done with information - (applies to medical and social security records).	
Personnel records				
Qualified privilege available to computer users (and informants).				
DPA's Jurisdiction				
To whom DPA answerable.				
DPA decisions appealable.				
Exemptions for police, national security.				
Trans-border data flow.				
Costs.			Unable to quantify but 'considerable'. 1976 - 60 million records. Estimated that enquiry service involving 5% of records would need 1300 more staff, capital of £1 million and annual costs of £8.5 million.	
Legalisation to cover manual systems also.		Points out that legislation for computers could create anomalies	Artificial to distinguish them	

Northern Ireland Office	Office of Population Census and Surveys	Scottish Home and Health Department	
NI (DHSS) support DHSS in London. Also said urgent need for more information which linkable between health and social services.	Strongly in favour of linkage for statistics purposes. But because of public fears, recommend notification to DPA.	Complex reply to this.	*Transfer of information by third parties and not subject in person.*
	No disclosure to subject for medical records. Disclosure in accordance with MRC article to researchers ie w/o consent.	Yes — re medical, also linkage important, both for care of individual and research.	*Exceptions to disclosure for medical and social work records.*
		Support CCA reply.	*Personnel records.*
		Defer to Lord Chancellor's submission.	*Qualified privilege available to computer users (and informants).*
	(Should include medical member(s)).		*DPA's jurisdiction.*
			To whom DPA answerable.
	Yes — if registration/licensing approach adopted.		*DPA decisions appealable.*
Want to reserve position regarding access to any data where security paramount.		Yes, in regard to all police systems holding personal information.	*Exemptions for police, national security.*
			Trans-border data flow.
			Costs
All remarks in p.34 apply with equal force to manual systems.	General principles concerning privacy and confidentiality apply equally to computers and manual systems.	Medical records should not be treated differently depending on what medium is.	*Legislation to cover manual systems also.*

2. Health Authorities and Other Medical Bodies

North Western RHA	Oxford RHA	South-West Thames RHA	South Western RHA	
No - Doctors should control.	No - Doctors should control;	No	No - (not to complete record anyway)	*Medical records - subject access.*
Favour non-identification. Keeping names off HAA, MHE. Want NHS number used on all medical records.	Research must not be hampered. Either exemption for it, or it should be included in purpose of collection of data.	Support MRC statement on research. (see BMJ 27/1/73)	Release of identifiable information for research only if - research approved by ethical body - authors of data agree -subject consents of is bypassed if prejudice to him by knowing of research.	*Medical records - statistics/research.*
Want linkage, eg of personnel with HAA to monitor resource utilisation.				*Medical records - linkage*
Individual consent impracticable suggest DPA could grant consent.	Individual consent impracticable.	Doctors must exchange freely without consent. Otherwise no transfer without agreement of doctor and patients consent.	Not unless data unidentifiable or subject consents or transfer in accordance with publicly debated and DPA endorsed rules.	*Medical records - transfer by 3rd party: consent?*
Para 37 (1) preferable.			Needs to be licensing/registration body and also a law enforcement body.	*Para 37 (1): DPA to be registration/licensing or Para 37 (2)-information gathering, investigating compaints and publishing findings.*
		"That which relates to an individual and which if made known to other persons would influence his future".	Very long and specific definition.	*How should personal information be defined?*
Not felt that RHA's need protection. Thought that bodies corporate would be covered unless provision to contrary.		NHS information should not pass outside NHS. Data held by associations etc. to be protected to extent nothing on individuals to be extractable.	YES	*Protection for corporate bodies and associations.*
Difficult to define how long to keep it. In principle, medical information of value forever.		Accepted		*The information should be kept only for as long as it is needed.*

Wessex RHA	Yorkshire RHA	DHSS (Health).	Scottish Home & Health Department (Health)	
No	No - Doctors should control;	No	No	*Medical records - subject access*
Worried in case research and management hampered. Ethical committee system satisfactory.		Impracticable to seek doctor's individual consent.		*Medical records - statistics/research.*
	Keen on linking with local authority.		Necessary within health system. Also linkage of medical and other vital events.	*Medical records - linkage.*
		Except for research, consent of doctor required, who should normally approach patient.	A doctor is designated 'holder' of information. His consent is required.	*Medical records - transfer by 3rd party: consent?*
				Para 37 (1): DPA to be registration/licensing or Para 37 (2)-information gathering, investigating complaints and publishing findings.
	"That information pertaining to an individual by which that individual can be identified by a 3rd party".			*How should personal information be defined?*
	Yes			*Protection for corporate bodies and associations.*
				The information should be kept only for as long as it is needed.

	Dr. M.A. Heasman Director Information Services Division. Scotish Home & Health Dept.	Dr. J. Baldwin Oxford Record Linkage Study	BMA	Hospital Consultants & Specialists Association
Medical Records - subject access.	No	No - Doctors should control;	No - (not to whole record anyway)	Want statutory right for patient to nominate doctor to see all information in patients name.
Medical records - statistics/research.	ISD operates large data bank containing identifiable data. Identification essential. Individual consent impracticable.		Concerned about identifiable information held in data banks.	Concerned about HAA, MHE, Oxford linkage. Feel identifiable information should be exception not rule.
Medical records - linkage.	Linkage necessary in ISD data bank to relate events to person.			Worried about linkage with non medical systems.
Medical records - transfer by 3rd party: consent?	Control of release of information from data bank vested in Director (to 1976).		Research aside, consent of doctor and patient required.	Consent of doctor in charge of patient should be necessary. (except for HAA)
Para 37 (1): DPA to be registration/licensing or Para 37 (2)-information gathering, investigating complaints and publishing findings.				Registration/Licensing.
How should personal information be defined?			"Medical record - any doct. on which information about a person in a professional relationship with a doctor is recorded".	All medical and medico-social material which identifies an individual.
Protection for corporate bodies and associations.			Should cover Medical Associations and medical defence bodies.	
The information should be kept only for as long as it is needed.			Agreed. But they think in terms of a number of years after death.	

184

Royal College of General Practitioners.	British Psychological Society	Patients Association	MIND	
No	Yes	No. Although felt, doctors often unnecessarily and unjustifiably refuse access. Want appeal to DPA.	Not if doctors think damaging, but put onus on doctors. Exceptions should be few.	*Medical records - subject access.*
Want to create distinction between primary (i.e. identifiable) and secondary data and presumably use secondary for research	Want to recognise right of individuals not to be included. Concerned about medical research and multi-nationals.			*Medical records - statistics/research.*
	Linkage undesirable. Advantage to research workers overridden by ethical objections.	Supports link between NHS and Social Services, but wants separate records.	Concerned about linkage generally.	*Medical records - linkage.*
			Consent of subject should be needed.	*Medical records - transfer by 3rd party: consent?*
	Licensing/registration.	Full registration/licensing of medical records systems undesirable because cost. But want registration with statutory body with power to strike off.	Licensing/registration but powers of investigation required	*Para 37 (1): DPA to be registration/licensing or Para 37 (2): information gathering, investigating complaints and publishing findings.*
Information given to a professional person in reasonable belief such information would be held in confidence in accordance with ethical standards of organisation.	"Information which uniquely identifies an individual".		"information about identifiable individuals" but there are grades of such information.	*How should personal information be defined?*
Only so far as "privileged" information can be linked to an individual.	Yes.		Confusion exists about privacy for individuals and organisations. Individuals privacy should not be delayed by technical problems.	*Protection for corporate bodies and associations.*
				The information should be kept only for as long as it is needed.

North-Western RHA	Oxford RHA	South-West Thames RHA	South-Western RHA	
Those held by health authorities should be treated in same way as medical records.		Standards should be no lower than for medical records.	Should be subject to same standards as medical records.	*Social work records.*
Feel staff appraisal should be open to subject, but not references. Currently basic information not open if in computer but RHA not opposed to openness.		Health records not to be disclosed without consent of doctor and employee.	Stringent (equal to those for medical records) rules needed for access and disclosure.	*Personnel records.*
		Yes	Question needs clarification	*Qualified privilege available to computer user (and informant)?*
No exemptions for health authorities.		"No groups should be excluded -either operator or user. Consult GMC.	Medical records must be within jurisdiction, but special rules necessary. Exemptions granted by DPA	*DPA's jurisdiction.*
		"The Privy Council - emphatically not the government of the day".	Parliament - direct.	*To whom should DPA be answerable?*
		Yes - through courts by injured party.	On points of law only.	*Should DPA's decisions be appealable?*
			Exemptions should be explicit in legislation or granted by DPA (latter preferred). Transfer of information from non exempt to exempt system needs approval of DPA.	*Exemption for police, national security.*
Not possible to quantify, but could be formidable for existing systems.	Significant extra costs if subjects allowed access to data.			*Costs.*
		Yes.		*Should legislation cover manual systems also?*

Wessex RHA	Yorkshire RHA	DHSS (Health)	Scottish Home and Health Department (Health)	
				Social work records.
	Open to subject except references in confidence and occupational health records. Control disclosure to 3rd parties.			Personnel records.
				Qualified privilege available to computer user (and informant)?
	Should include health records.	Want exemption for medical records from regulations regarding access, disclosure and notification of transfer.		DPA's jurisdiction.
	Parliament.			To whom should DPA be answerable?
				Should DPA's decisions be appealable?
				Exemption for police, national security.
	1976 seminar:- 10/15% staffing, 5/10% capacity reduction. Existing systems a major problem.	Excessive	Considerable	Costs.
Computer files same in essence as manual files.	Yes - inconsistent if not.	Sees inconsistency, so agrees computer systems should conform to manual standards.	Appears to be no reason to treat differently in the disclosure of information to subject or transfer to 3rd party.	Should legislation cover manual systems also?

	Dr M.A. Heasman Director of Information Services Division Scottish Home and Health Dept.	Dr J.A. Baldwin Oxford Record Linkage Study	BMA	Hospital Consultants and Specialists Association
Social work records.			As for medical records, would restrict subject access.	
Personnel records.			NHS as employer should have no access to employee medical records.	
Qualified privilege available to computer user (and informant)?			Computers irrelevant. Law applicable whatever the recording medium.	
DPA's jurisdiction.	Health data banks should be within DPA's jurisdiction. Maybe health DPA required.	GMC should control ethical practice in regard to medical records.	Medical records must be within jurisdiction.	
To whom should DPA be answerable?	Regarding health data banks: DPA must be independent of health service and government.		Minister, but parliamentary commissioner to be closely involved.	(Government nominated, but concerned about executive power.)
Should DPA's decisions be appealable?			No	
Exemption for police, national security.			No exemptions to police in regard to access to medical data.	
Costs.	Might be considerable			
Should legislation cover manual systems also?				

Royal College of General Practitioners.	British Psychological Society	Patients Association	MIND	
Observations on medical records apply equally to social services records.	Open to subject.		All social work records should be available to subject.	*Social work records.*
			Restriction only when access limited to author. References should be available.	*Personnel records.*
Yes			No, but have another proposed defence for person transmitting information bona fide and reasonably believing it true.	*Qualified privilege available to computer user (and informant)?*
All primary computer files and users should be within jurisdiction.	Need supervision from outside any given profession.		Private and public data banks holding information on more than 10,000 individuals.	*Private and public data banks holding DPA's jurisdiction.*
"Parliament (Home Secretary?)"	Parliamentary Commissioner (or DPA should have equivalent status).		Lord Chancellor's Department.	*To whom should DPA be answerable?*
Yes: to "Parliament (Home Secretary?)".			Yes: to divisional court of QBD by subject or another.	*Should DPA's decisions be appealable?*
				Exemption for police, national security.
	May become prohibitive unless limitation on security required. But any new system must include costs due to legislation in cost of system. Problems for existing systems.			*Costs.*
	Same problems in both.			*Should legislation cover manual systems also?*

3. Lamsac
    Police
    Post Office

    NCCL
    Justice
    All Party Committee for Freedom of Information

    British Computer Society
    DPMA
    ICL
    NCC

Local Authorities Management Services and Computer Committee.	Police Home Office Evidence	Police Metropolitan Police	Post Office	
Detailed statements impractical. Suggest production of public documents giving categories of data, how used, who has access, where further information available.	Could be met in broad terms, but publication of details of scope of system would defeat their object.			*Para 34: Existence and purpose of information systems holding personal data in computers, use made of data and which interests have access to be publicly known.*
Changes in purpose or use made known by public advertisements or notification to DPA.	Could be met in general terms provided broad definition of purpose (e.g. prevention and detection of crime).	Purpose should be broadly defined: "to assist the maintenance of public order".		*Para 34: Information not to be used for purpose other than that for which given without consent of subject or other authorised justification.*
			P.O agrees with p.34 principles, but warns against:- — excessive costs — hindering of prudent business practice — hindering technical development — creating overwhelming demand for information requests.	*Para 34: Only personal information necessary for declared purposes should be collected.*
Operator should be local authority in corporate sense. Impossible to guarantee accuracy	Cannot be met for police systems.	Not possible to guarantee accuracy of some information.		*Para 34: Operator of system to be responsible for ensuring accuracy and relevance of information.*
Yes - but limited to factual information i.e. excluding subjective data. Proof of identification needed.	Cannot be met for police systems.	Not for operational records. For criminal records: problems of cost and identification of enquirer.		*Para 34: Subject to be able to check relevance and accuracy and correct.*
If to be identified in detail, then enormous cost and inconvenience.	Cannot be met for police systems.			*Para 34: Subject to be able to find out what done with information and to whom given.*
Should be responsibility of user to specify time		CRO and fingerprint systems carefully weeded. Criminal intelligence would be hampered by this.		*Para 34: Information to be kept only for as long as it is needed.*
Should be responsibility of user departments.		Identities separated from rest of data in Metropolitan statistics.		*Para 34: Safeguards needed to ensure statistics presented in way which doesn't reveal details of identifiable individual.*
p.37(2) preferred because 37(1) impracticable, costly, and would impede computer developments initially.		Licensing 13,000+ systems would be immense task. Police do not want burden of prosecuting under privacy legislation.	p37(1) - costly and involving huge effort. Prefers p37(2) but with greater powers to prevent abuse.	*Para 37 (1) - registration/licensing or Para 37 (2) - information gathering, investigating complaints and publishing findings.*
Lengthy definition produced.			Definition should not be too narrow -will go out of date.	*What is a computer?*
Name, address, sex, marital status, age should be public. Personal information then is personal characteristics, habits, description, beliefs achievements etc.		"Any direct or associated information about subject relevant to purpose for which record kept".	Should be given widest possible connotation consistent with direct relevance to individual or organisation.	*How should personal information be defined?*
Difficult to see how could apply to local authorities. Generally unnecessary to give associations/bodies same protection as			No distinction should be made between these and individuals.	*Protection for associations and corporate bodies.*

	...limited to Public sector)	
Yes, Register(s) of data banks required, specifying the information mentioned.	Yes. Publish in Gazette.	*Para 34: Existence and purpose of information systems holding personal data in computers, use made of data and which interests have access to be publicly known.*
Yes. Statutory authorisation only justified when public interest overrides principle of individual consent.	Yes. Also publish new use in Gazette and allow public debate.	*Para 34: Information not to be used for purpose other than that for which given without consent of subject or other authorised justification.*
Yes. Concerned at amount of irrelevant information gathered.	Yes. Relevant to accomplish a purpose of Organ of Public Administration which required by statute.	*Para 34: Only personal information necessary for declared purposes should be collected.*
	Responsibility on Organ of P. Administration primarily.	*Para 34: Operator of system to be responsible for ensuring accuracy and relevance of information.*
Yes. (with very few exceptions). Care needed to identify inquirer.	Yes. Administrative review procedure if dispute about correction with appeal to courts.	*Para 34: Subject to be able to check relevance and accuracy and correct.*
Yes. Individuals should be given trace on request (except possibly for routine uses).	Yes. Log should be kept.	*Para 34: Subject to be able to find out what done with information and to whom given.*
Yes. information should be regularly up-dated or destroyed.	Yes.	*Para 34: Information to be kept only for as long as it is needed.*
Yes. In case of research files, data and name files should be separate.	Transfer to statistics/research in non-identifiable form	*Para 34: Safeguards needed to ensure statistics presented in way which doesn't reveal details of identifiable individual.*
Para 37(1) is only acceptable alternative.	Para 37(1) (refusal or revocation of license gives teeth).	*Para 37(1) - registration/licensing or para 37(2) - information gathering, investigating complaints and publishing findings.*
Definition must be wide enough to cover any autotmatic system.	Better to define information systems.	*What is a computer?*
Widely. Any information which can be identified with an individual.	See draft Freedom of Information and Privacy Bill.	*How should personal information be defined?*
Protection needed for partnerships and organisations where information could be linked with identifiable individuals.	Yes	*Protection for associations and corporate bodies.*

193

British Computer Society	Data Processing Managment Association	International Computers Ltd	National Computing Centre	
Standard form and place of publication of this required. DPA could publish list annually.				*Para 34:* *Existence and purpose of information systems holding personal data in computers, use made of data and which interests have access to be publicly known.*
Supported, but 'other authorised justification' is vague. Basis of authority and control must be clearly specified.				*Para 34:* *Information not to be used for purpose other than that for which given without consent of subject or other authorised justification.*
Mechanism needed for resolving disagreements about what necessary.				*Para 34:* *Only personal information necessary for declared purposes should be collected.*
Problem in defining operator. Also responsibility should be limited to that reasonable in terms of cost and effort.		'Operator' imprecise. Impossible to guarantee 100% accuracy.		*Para 34:* *Operator of system to be responsible for ensuring accuracy and relevance of information.*
Could be very expensive.		No technical problem, but problems of cost and enquirer's identity.		*Para 34:* *Subject to be able to check relevance and accuracy and correct.*
Could be costly to maintain log of all usage and make available on request.		Detailed log impracticable.		*Para 34:* *Subject to be able to find out what done with information and to whom given.*
'Need' to be defined.		Personal information may be in archived files, and over time its sensitivity may change.		*Para 34:* *Information to be kept only for as long as it is needed.*
				Para 34: *Safeguards needed to ensure statistics presented in way which doesn't reveal details of identifiable individual.*
		Both (need to monitor registered systems).	License sensitive systems, register all systems, DPA needs powers of inspection.	*Para 37 (1) - registration/licensing or Para 37 (2) - information gathering, investigating complaints and publishing findings.*
	Any definition soon outmoded.	Emphasize information system, not hardware.	Avoid hardware definitions.	*What is a computer?*
		(Level of control should be related to sensitivity).		*How should personal information be defined?*
Almost impossible to draft appropriate statute.	Yes		Yes	*Protection for associations and corporate bodies.*

Subjective information to be labelled as such. Do not restrict transfer within Local Authorities.			Non-statistics information should not be transferred unless - required by law - or law would recognise duty - or subject consents.	*Transfer of information by third parties and not subject in person.*
Med - presume public support for exception. Social work - want to restrict access to subjective data.				*Exceptions to disclosure for medical and social work records.*
No problem with factual data. But restrict access to opinions, references, subjective data.		In 1976, most still manual. Copies of individual police officers record shown to him.	Factual information may be released to subject. Opposes access to information about performance promotability etc not because by nature undisclosable, but because needs interpreting.	*Personnel records.*
Should be some privilege or protection available to employers of computer staff or users.			Yes.	*Qualified privilege available to computer user (and informant).*
Private and public sectors and directed at corporate organisations holding data, not individual operatives of organisations.			All users of computers in UK, Channel Islands and Isle of Man which process personal information.	*DPA's jurisdiction.*
Report to government, but answerable to no-one. Local Government representation on DPA required. Other reps:- professionals and others government thinks appropriate.			"To Department of State would appear logical".	*To whom DPA answerable.*
Not necessary if p37(2) adopted.			Yes, and to a specialist tribunal if it is a registration authority.	*Yes, and to a specialist tribunal if it is DPA's decisions appealable?*
Police systems - yes. Question of police access to other systems without consent must be considered. Local Authorities computers used for national security need exemption.	Yes - on Home Secretary's certificate. System should be exempt from purview of DPA.			*Exemptions for police, national security.*
	Yes - for exempted systems as above. Safeguards specified by Home Secretary.			*Special safeguards for police systems.*
Some Local Authorities use US computers. Controls must cover transfer of information cross-border.			Draw attention to work of OECD and CEPT work on data flow.	*Trans-border data flow.*
"enormous" costs of idealistic rather than practical legislation. No estimate possible.		Concerned at cost of disclosing criminal records to subjects.	1976 estimate for PO - initial cost of £750,000, annual £500,000 on basis 2% customer 10% staff enquire annually.	*Costs.*
Same considerations apply. Inequitable to treat them differently.		If undue restrictions on computer systems, then would use manual.		*Legislation to cover manual systems also?*

National Council for Civil Liberties	Justice	All Party Committee for Freedom of Information and Privacy (Comments limited to Public sector)	
No. If patient prepared to ask, he takes risk of finding unpleasant information.	Special arrangements needed for information supplied by third parties, because inherently more inaccurate, irrelevant out of date etc.	Need consent of subject (certain defined exceptions).	*Transfer of information by third parties and not subject in person.*
	Medical - possibly. Social Work - No.	Medical records available to patient via own doctor. Social work - no different to other government records.	*Exceptions to disclosure for medical and social work records.*
Should be open (including references) to employee.	Powers of DPA should extend to these.	As for social work records i.e. provision of draft bill re disclosure etc should apply.	*Personnel records.*
Yes, but extend legal aid to defamation actions.	No, at least no more than it may apply by reason of present law.	No point in having statutory provision. Rely on current law (also remedy in bill).	*Qualified privilege available to computer user (and informant).*
	Private and public information systems in UK all users.	(Note*: given draft bill, thought DPA unnecessary.)	*DPA's jurisdiction*
	Parliament through P.M. or Home Secretary, but independence of paramount importance.	Parliamentary Commissioner (See note* above).	*To whom DPA answerable*
Licensing decisions should be appealable to courts or tribunal with further appeal on points of law.	Yes, on points of law or mixed fact and law to Divisional Court.	Yes to High Court (See note* above).	*DPA's decisions appealable?*
Only for intelligence systems. Even so should be within DPA jurisdiction.	Yes, statutorily defined. But report to DPA required annually.	See draft bill.	*Exemptions for police, national security.*
		Only if - subject consents, or -emergency or - same protection available.	*Special safeguards for police systems.*
Statutory controls required. Should cover off-shore data banks. Export of information only with individuals consent.	Control required.		*Trans-border data flow.*
Concerned that safeguards be denied because of cost. If safeguards make system economically unviable, don't store data.		Obviously initial costs, but savings in improvement to government efficiency as result of legislation.	*Costs*
Yes		Yes	*Legislation to cover manual systems also?*

British Computer Society	Data Processing Management Association	ICL	NCC	
Controls must take account of free flow of information in a democracy i.e. no censorship.	Only with subjects consent Implied consent for doctors. Exemptions for court.	No restrictions on transfer of non-sensitive information for normal business purposes.	Need to distinguish fact from opinion.	*Transfer of information by third parties and not subject in person.*
Not competent to judge. but concerned about extent and limits of exceptions.	Medical - problems: maybe patient should see.		Majority-favour restriction. Large minority - favour openness.	*Exceptions to disclosure for medical and social work records.*
	Factual data should be disclosed. Balance required in regard to judgemental data. Case-law to develop to govern this.		Majority view - restrict subject access to management information. Large minority - against restrictions.	*Personnel records.*
			Yes.	*Qualified privilege available to computer user (and informant).*
All data banks subject to specific exemptions.		Public and private sectors.	All systems, public and private.	*DPA's jurisdiction.*
Independent of political and civil service control and so answerable to			Must be independent from political and financial pressures.	*To whom DPA answerable.*
Yes - Courts	Yes - Courts	To High Court on points of law. On technical and policy matters: no.	Yes	*DPA's decisions appealable?*
Yes.	Yes - but aware of possible abuses.	Yes, but specific systems known to DPA. No exemption for transfers from non-exempt systems.	Yes - but still register with DPA.	*Exemptions for police, national security.*
				Special safeguards for police systems.
Complex issue - investigating further (1976).		Hard to prevent avoidance of legislations. But seek agreement internationally.	Further study needed (1976).	*Trans-border data flow.*
Have estimated direct costs of a licensing/registration DPA 1976 - min ½ million.	DPA direct costs insignificant in comparison to costs within installations.	Design and operational costs of safeguards likely to be greater than 5%.	Could be high.	*Costs.*
Yes.	Yes.	Yes.	Yes.	*Legislation to cover manual systems also?*

APPENDIX B
PARTICIPANTS AT THE CONFERENCE

Speakers and workshop leaders

Alan Benjamin	Director General, Computing Services Association
Lord Boston of Faversham	Minister of State, Home Office
Michael Bruce	Manpower Adviser, British Airways
Tony Bunyan	Director, State Research
Edward Cluff	General Secretary, Institute of Data Processing Management
Dr John Dawson	Assistant Secretary, British Medical Association
Trudy Hayden	Former Director, Privacy Project, American Civil Liberties Union
Joe Jacob	Lecturer in Law, London School of Economics
Rory Johnston	Journalist, *Computer Weekly*
Ron Lacey	Social Work Adviser, MIND
Sir Norman Lindop	Chairman, Data Protection Committee
John McNulty	Managing Director, General Robots
Russell Pipe	Editor, *Transnational Data Report*
Charles Read	Director, Inter-Bank Research Organisation
Professor Paul Samet	Director, University of London Computing Centre
Hugh Screen	Deputy Director, LAMSAC
Barry Sherman	Director of Research, ASTMS
Paul Sieghart	Member, Data Protection Committee
Rt Hon David Steel MP	Leader, Liberal Party
Rabbe Wrede	Head, Administrative Division, Data Inspection Board, Stockholm

Chairmen of Sessions

Lord Avebury	Chairman, Digico Ltd
Edward Cluff	General Secretary, Institute of Data Processing Management
Sir Norman Lindop	Chairman, Data Protection Committee
Paul Sieghart	Member, Data Protection Committee

Delegates

Access	M.Hawkins
	B.M.Williams
Advisory Centre for Education	Peter Newell
AEUW TASS	Ian Benson
Age Concern England	Judith A.Walker
American Express	P.J.Hall
	R.C.Law
Argyll & Clyde Health Area	Dr J.S.Bryden
Associated Society of Locomotive Engineers and Firemen	N.Milligan
Bank of England	T.P.Sweeney
Bank of Scotland	M.N.McTaggart
Birmingham City Council	Cllr.N.Hargreaves
	Cllr.A.M.Rydge
BL Cars Data Centre	G.P.Parr
BP Trading Ltd	P.E.Hook
British Bankers Association	N.C.Cannon
	J.M.Evans
British Psychological Society	Dr H.Brierley
Burmah-Castrol Company	P.H.Crosby
	P.H.Groves
Burton Group	J.E.Shaw Phillips
Commission for Racial Equality	Francis Deutsch
Consumer's Association	Jeanette Attan
	Roger Cozens
Co-operative Bank Ltd.	H.W.H.Sheppard
Corporation of Lloyd's	T.A.Barton
Council of Europe	Frits W.Hondius
Credit Data Ltd.	P.F.Standish Brooks
Deloitte Haskins & Sells	W.H.Buckley
	E.T.Peers
Dept. of Health & Social Security	Dr A.Fenton Lewis
Dept. of Industry, CSE Department	Leslie Huckfield, MP
	B.R.Taylor

Derbyshire Area Health Authority	D.Harrison
Esso Petroleum Company Ltd.	Miss S.J.Tait
Gesellschaft fur Mathematik und	Herbert Burkert
Datenverarbeitung	
Health Visitors Association	Joan Hudson
Home Office	R.A.Harrington
	T.M.Harris
	Ralph Shuffley
IBM Europe S.A.	J.Keith Williams
IBM UK Limited	R.A.Barber
I.C.I.	J.Boggon
	B.Buckroyd
ICLCUA, University of Strathclyde	S.A. Goold
	Dr R. Kingslake
Inland Revenue	Brian A.Mace
Justice	Tom Sargant
LAMSAC	I.Robertson
	H.Screen
The Littlewoods Organisation Ltd.	P.Chalk
	P.Slater
Lloyds Bank Ltd. Access Dept.	M.J.Gale
Lloyds Bank Ltd. Management Services Div.	D.E.Humphrey
London Borough of Greenwich	L.Bedford
	D.Trim
Lucas Group Computing	Alan McEntee
Medical Protection Society	Dr Duncan Murray
Midland Bank Ltd.	I.R.F.Cameron
	T.M.Hollis
	W.D.Jarman
	P.E.J.Lyon
	H.A.Meyer
	D.Whitworth
	E.C.Woods
H.D.Miller MP	
MIND, National Assoc. for Mental Health	Tony Smythe
NALGO	John Thane
National Computing Centre Ltd.	Hugh Pitcher
National Westminster Bank Ltd.	B.S.Washington
NCCL	William Birtles
	Ruth Cohen
	Patricia Hewitt
	Alan Hicks
	Roland Jeffery
NUM (COSA)	L.D.Story

PACTEL-PA Computers &
Telecommunications   R.Hughesdon
Patients Association   Dame Elizabeth Ackroyd
                                       Mrs Moira Tanner
Plessey Co.Ltd.   Gavin Morrison
Police — Merseyside   Clive Dawson
                                       James Sloan
Police — Northumbria   S.E.Bailey
                                       Paul B.Whitehouse
Police Staff College, Bramshill   Chief Supt. Alan Dyer
Outer Circle Policy Unit   James Cornford
                                       Jason Ditton
Post Office   D.J.Powell
Post Office Data Processing Service   J.P.Bossman
Jo Richardson MP
Royal Insurance Co.Ltd.   P.J.L.Keffler
Royal Statistical Society   H.P.Wynn
SCICON   David J.Dent
Shell UK Oil   A.Byrne
                                       Mrs P.Collins
                                       J.C.M.Davies
                                       C.J.Evans
State Research   Sarah Harrison
W.H.Smith & Son Ltd.   Philip Done
Social Services Association   G.Lythe
Socialist Medical Association   John Holliday
Standard Telephones & Cables Ltd.   D.G.Carpenter
Trent Regional Health Authority   J.W.Payton
TSB Computer Services Ltd.   G.W.C.Hayes
U.A.P.T. Ltd.   Dr B.W.Bailey
UI Management Consultants Ltd.   Dr R.V.Austin
UK Atomic Energy Authority   Cdr. F.Bromilow
Wiltshire County Council   E.J.S.Gregory